LLANDEGLA

THEN AND NOW

LLANDEGLA MILLENNIUM
ACTION GROUP

St. Tecla's Church, Llandegla,
drawn by Carl Hellyn, the village postman.

Copyright	The Llandegla Millennium Action Group, 2003 Copyright of all photographs and illustrations also resides with their owners.
Published by:	The Llandegla Millennium Action Group, Llandegla Memorial Hall, Llandegla, Wrexham, North Wales LL11 3AW
Printed by:	Printcentre Wales Limited, Mold/Yr Wyddgrug, Flintshire, North Wales CH7 1HA
Cover design:	Anne Robinson
Technical editors:	Fleur Davies and Janet Strivens
Editor:	Phil Clark

ISBN: 0-9545211-0-2

Acknowledgement: The Llandegla Millennium Action Group
gratefully acknowledges the funding from the Heritage Lottery Fund
which made the publication of this book possible.

Front cover illustration: Llandegla Village, a linocut taken from a photograph, 1900.
Drawn by Anne Robinson.

Back cover illustration: The Llandegla Bridge, 2002.
Drawn by Carl Hellyn, the village postman.

Editor's note: An acknowledgement is provided for each illustration. Every effort has been made to ensure that these are correct. Should any error or infringement of copyright have inadvertently occurred, the publishers will be pleased to rectify matters at the earliest opportunity. The quality of some of the photographs may seem to be inferior by today's standards, but some of these are very old (a few around a hundred years) and there is a limit to the enhancement of quality that can be achieved by modern technology. The contents are as factual as can reasonably be ascertained, but it would be most useful to be told both about any inaccuracies that may have occurred, and about further items that could (or perhaps should!) have been included. Such information will be invaluable if a second edition is prepared.

Maps that are based on Ordnance Survey maps have been drawn up with permission of The Controller of Her Majesty's Stationery Office, Crown Copyright MC 100033837.

Locations given as 'to the left', and 'to the right' are as you leave the centre of the village, unless specifically described.

'Parish' refers to the present parish boundaries after their considerable extension in the 1920's, even when discussing earlier times, unless otherwise noted.

Farmland.
A few points for those less familiar with the countryside. Some of the features mentioned in this book are on private land and with no access from a public footpath, such as St Tecla's Well (Court Farm) and Tomen y Rhodwydd (Castell Farm). Many of our local farms are family farms, so their fields are part of the homestead. It would therefore be a courtesy to seek permission before visiting, irrespective of any rights which there may be. This will engender goodwill and help to ensure a friendly reception for future visitors. While on farmland, do remember the country code. In particular, gates are shut to confine animals as the aftermath of a gate carelessly left open can be very expensive in both time and money - farms are businesses as well as homes. Also in view of the large number of sheep and pheasants locally, **all** dogs should always be kept on a lead.

Children of Llandegla
Primary School.
Right: Children with their
teacher Miss Gillian Edwards.
1971
Below: The junior recorder
group. 1971

Left: The school
was so full that classes
were taken in the
cloakroom. 1955

Contents

FOREWORD

The publication of this book to celebrate the millennium, 2000 AD, has given us the opportunity to wipe clean the window of time and age and look back. We in Llandegla are able to see traces of occupation reaching back to the birth of Christendom and the Roman presence here in the early years of the first millennium.

We can only imagine how our ancestors looked on what life was like through the centuries. Llandegla was for hundreds of years a centre for drovers who brought other influences, bringing a constant change in culture and practice. We have evidence that during at least the last two centuries the community was very self-sufficient, having its own baker, tailor, bootmaker, blacksmith and others who supplied the needs of the village. Though we may look back with nostalgia to the 'old days', there is no doubt that our forebears endured a great deal of hardship and poverty.

It is hoped that the text and photographs will revive memories of the past and will give pleasure to the many people who have some association with Llandegla.

William Owen,
Accre Hall
Llandegla

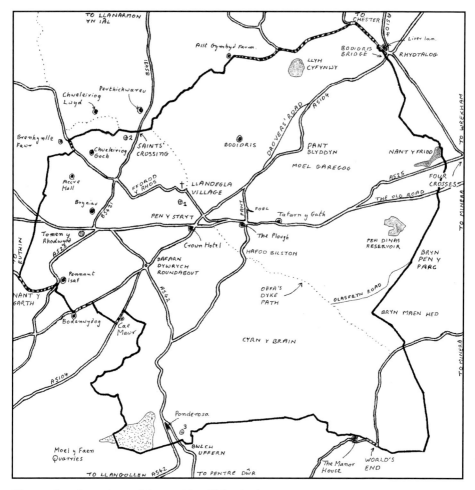

The modern boundary of the parish of Llandegla.

1. St Tecla's Well
2. St Garmon's Well
3. St Collen's Well

1. LLANDEGLA: VILLAGE AND PARISH

The village of Llandegla nestles in the valley of the young River Alyn, about four miles from the Horseshoe Pass, at about 850 feet (260m) above sea level. The Offa's Dyke walk runs through the length of the village on its way between Chepstow and Prestatyn. The parish of Llandegla covers about ten square miles, mostly farm land and moorland, with a population of around five hundred, including children.

Three Welsh words make up the name of this parish: LLAN, TECLA and (yn - 'in') IÂL, which gives Llandegla yn Iâl.

LLAN: This is an ancient celtic word meaning a place of ritual or worship. As time went by, it came to mean an enclosure set aside for the worship of the Christian God. Churches constructed of wood were built on the 'llan'. It is said that a church was established in Llandegla during the sixth century.

TECLA: St Tecla is the patron saint of our church (p.181). It is said that Saint Tecla was said to be a virgin converted by Paul during his travels (though there is little real evidence for her existence!) There are two conflicting tales about her. One says that she was martyred by Nero. Another says that she was on her way to Syria when she was set upon by men of 'evil intent'. Nearby was a rock which opened up and engulfed her safe from the ravages of men.

IÂL: The meaning of the word *Iâl* is cleared and cultivated land. It is opposite in meaning to the Welsh '*anIÂLwch*', i.e. the *anialwch* (dense forest growth) of Dyffryn Clwyd on one side and that of Dyffryn Maelor on the other.

Llandegla is a typical village in that it is made up of old cottages supplemented by a complement of modern houses. It has an atmosphere of permanence in contrast to the redevelopments that are occurring in the towns nearby, but it is itself changing as it continues to be shaped by events and life in the country as a whole. However it is still a working village in that many people living in the village work within the parish, often in farming, which contributes to the stability of community life.

Village life has always been subject to change as time passes, but in recent years the rate of change has become much more rapid, driven by

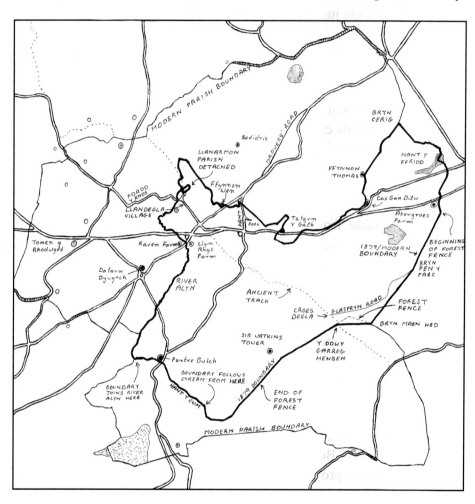

The old boundaries of Llandegla parish
[Scale: one mile from the Crown Hotel to Tafarn y Gâth]

Holy Wells   ⊕   Offa's Dyke (where off-road) ....

(based on the 2000 Explorer Ordnance Survey map by permission of Ordnance Survey on behalf of the Controller of Her Majesty's Stationary Office, @ Crown Copyright MC 100033837)

the ease of communication made available by modern innovations such as motor transport, television and the telephone (but not counting the bus service!) Llandegla just missed out on a railway during the railway age, which would have had a dramatic effect on the village. This greater ease of communication with the world outside - the movement of information, people and goods - has reduced the necessity for the old close interdependence within the village. Around a hundred years ago there were many tradesmen in the village serving the needs of the inhabitants, but now these needs can easily be satisfied from elsewhere. The village carpenter is now employed in a town nearby while window frames come into the village mass-produced from a factory miles away. However there are still products such as meat, potatoes and logs that are both produced and consumed in the village (and elsewhere). Some services are also available from within the village, such as property repairs, furniture manufacture, gardening and farm contracting. Farming was and still is the mainstay of the village economy, but in these modern times this is supplemented by the provision of food and accommodation for tourists and other visitors. All this is only a small proportion of the range of services that were needed in the village in the old days when travel was difficult for ordinary folk.

A further recent change in the mode of life in the village has centred around the role of the 'big house' - Bodidris. This house has a long history itself (described later), but formerly the owners of Bodidris owned much of Llandegla and the surrounding farmland. Now the farms have been sold and Bodidris itself is a hotel surrounded by only a few acres of its former property. In earlier times many of the inhabitants of the village would have worked, directly or indirectly, for Bodidris which therefore maintained a controlling and stabilising influence over life in the village, an influence that has now disappeared.

The parish boundaries

Llandegla became a parish around 1200 AD. Shortly after the First World War, the parish boundaries were greatly extended, taking in areas that were formerly parts of the parishes of Llantysilio and Llanarmon. The old Llandegla parish boundary is taken from the OS map of 1879. Generally the boundary follows streams or other natural features. Where these do not exist, hedgerows or lines of boundary stones are utilised. In some places the boundary marches across the middle of a field and then changes course with no apparent waymarks on the ground or other

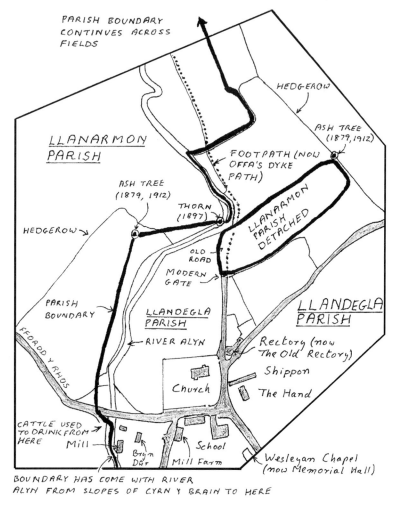

Detailed map of the route of the old parish boundary as it passes near to the village. Dates in brackets refer to the maps on which the trees are noted. The hedgerow at the top has gone, but there is an ash tree standing on its own in the field which could possibly be the one on the map. (*Redrawn by Phil Clark from the 1912 OS map*)

feature. This may be because the original waymark trees have rotted off or there has been a change of ownership of land. However, many a hedgerow has been *in situ* for hundreds of years, well beyond the normal lifespan of its constituent bushes.

A stream, Nant y Cwm, runs down the slope of Cyrn y Brain in a small steep valley. This was sufficiently conspicuous to form part of the parish boundary. The boundary followed this stream downhill, leaving it to pass through the Travellers' Rest Inn (now demolished), beside Pentre Bwlch Farm and then across fields to the River Alyn. It followed the River Alyn all the way to Llandegla, it even followed a few dried-up meanders on its way. It then followed a complicated course around Llandegla using trees,

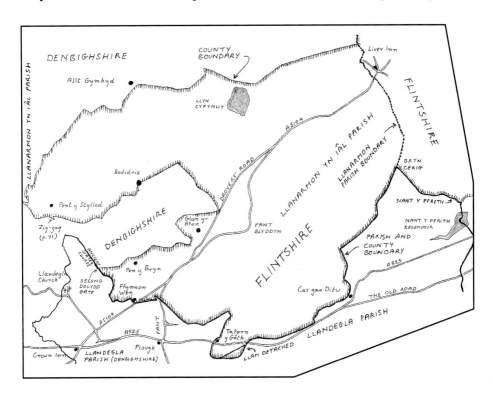

The parish of Llanarmon yn Iâl in Flintshire based on the 1879 OS map. This area is now incorporated into Llandegla parish in Denbighshire. The old county and parish boundaries follow the same line from Nant y Ffridd to the Second Dolydd Gate (*Redrawn by Phil Clark from the 1879 OS map*)

now gone, as boundary markers. The Llanarmon Parish detached is an anomaly, similar to those that affected country boundaries before reorganisation in 1974. The detached portion of Llanarmon was only part of a field, less than one and a half acres.

The boundary eventually passes through *Ffynnon Wen* (White Well). The farmhouse itself was in Llanarmon Parish in Flintshire, the outbuildings were in Llandegla parish in Denbighshire. (The well at Ffynnon Wen never dried up; during a drought people came from the village to this well for their water.) After crossing the A525, it picked up the stream Yr Alun Bach which it followed past the fish farm at Casgan Ditw (the fish ponds were not there then) up to and above Ffynnon Thomas, a convenient waymark.

The next feature was the Nant y Ffridd reservoir (then newly constructed) where the boundary followed the original stream bed under the water. It then went upstream under the A525 until it ran out of natural features. From there, until it again met the stream in the small steep valley, the boundary followed a series of straight lines over the featureless moor.

The old and the modern parish boundaries now follow the Llandegla Forest fence as far as Bryn Maen Hedd. Formerly the boundary was marked by boundary stones (large rocks) or heaps of stones. There is one of these stones by the stile at Pen y Parc. There are now no obvious features to mark Bryn Maen Hed where the parishes of Llandegla, Llangollen and Wrexham used to meet: once it was marked by a heap of stones. The forest fence diverges from the old parish boundary between here and *Y Ddwy Garreg Henben* (The Two Old Top Rocks) where the Offa's Dyke path (p. 130) enters the forest. The rocks seem to have gone also, though they were there in 1812. This diversion was probably to avoid a boggy bit (it is a *very* boggy bit!). *Croes Degla* (Tegla's Cross) is where the Glasfryn road between Minera and Moel y Faen used to cross the old track which is now the Offa's Dyke path. In the map of 1740 it is noted as the location of a 'great stone'. The Reverend D.R.Thomas writing in 1874 says, "Croes Tecla formerly stood on the borders of Llangollen parish". Could this have been a waymark at the crossroads or part of an ancient cross which has now gone missing?

There were eleven boundary stones that used to mark the old parish boundary between the end of the forest fence and the stream, Nant y Cwm. Now only two are easily seen, one above the elbow on the road to the radio masts, the other by the end of the forest fence. The corner post here is supported by a part of the old radar mast (pp. 65, 129). Two other pieces of radar mast are concreted into the ground near to the second (smaller) radio mast, exactly in line with the old parish boundary.

The modern boundary of the parish is taken from the OS Explorer map, published in 2000. As before, this also features on the ground as far as possible. For example, after leaving the stream at Rhydtalog the boundary follows the road all the way to Allt Gymbyd Farm. Since the 1989 Pathfinder map, the boundary around Cae Mawr and Bodanwydog now follows existing fence lines instead of wandering across fields. Also, it has at last been changed to go on dry land around Nant y Ffridd reservoir instead of through it.

An area along the northern parish boundary going west, but more into Llanarmon Parish, is known locally as the 'Abbey Lands', a relic of former ownership (p.25).

Though further minor changes may be made to the boundary in the future to accommodate changes in the countryside, one hopes that the value of the integrity of the parish boundary will continue to be recognised. By providing a sense of belonging for those that live within it, it is a cohesive influence that helps to keep the community together.

Llandegla today

The village is a mix of people whose roots lie in Llandegla and incomers whose roots lie elsewhere. Over three dozen houses have been built since the 1970's. Only five of these are occupied by someone who is native to

The Population of Llandegla from 1801 to 1991

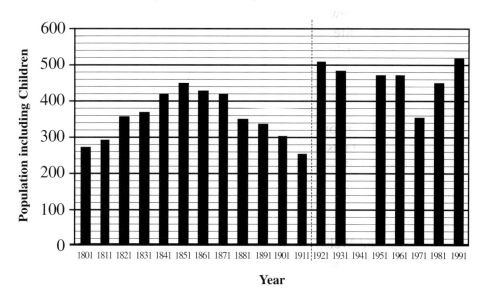

Between 1911 and 1921 the Parish was much enlarged, hence the increase in numbers. There was no census in 1941 because of the war.

the area, the rest have come from outside. This immigration was encouraged in the 1970's as it was felt that the village had either to expand or die - the village school and shop would have been in danger of closing. This decline in the numbers of villagers between the 1960's and the 1970's can be seen from the census returns above.

Many incomers embrace village life with enthusiasm but they inevitably lack the actual experiences of the past which explain why the present is as it is, so tradition can easily become lost. This book records some aspects of this fragile history before its understanding, and the people that were part of it, pass away for ever.

People have moved into Llandegla either to retire or to improve their quality of life while still working. Many settle in and become part of the village. Others miss the facilities of a town and become impatient of the need to travel to work and visit friends, and so move out after a few years. Such people miss out on much that village life has to offer. This is also unfortunate in that it leads to a greater turnover of inhabitants, particularly in the new estates, so reducing the social stability which is a feature of village life. In the past this stability was due to the relative isolation from outside influences and also the way in which the inhabitants knew each other so well - at school together, working together, possibly related, and so on. With the exodus of younger people and increase in outside influence, this stability is threatened with decline. This is where the incomers can be crucial to the survival of village life. If the new inhabitants look upon their arrival more as joining a very extended family rather than just moving to a nice pad in the countryside, both they and the village as a whole will benefit from the increase in vigour of village life.

Both English and Welsh are spoken in Llandegla, the latter particularly among the farming community. Less Welsh is spoken now as compared with former times, as Welsh speakers move out to find work, due to the general decline in the number of people employed in agriculture, and English people move in from over the border. However there is a rich social life among the Welsh community, aspects of which are described later (pp. 201, 203). In addition, a number of people who have moved into the area are taking an active interest in Welsh as part of our social heritage and as a medium for communication.

Llandegla has had a long past and is set to have a good future. The village has changed over the years and will continue to change. It is up to ourselves at the present time situated between the past and the future to ensure that further change enhances future life for Llandegla.

2. AS WE WERE: EARLY BEGINNINGS

New Stone Age cave dwellers

As 'Iâl' is a name of great antiquity, it is perhaps not surprising that traces of prehistoric man having roamed and lived in this locality have been found.

Charles Darwin (of evolution fame) had been sent a small box of bones that he passed onto Professor Boyd Dawkins. These bones had been washed by rain from an adjacent neolithic midden, of which there is now no trace, at Perthichwareu. Prof. Dawkins was then stimulated to investigate three caves nearby (in 1869-72). When excavated, these caves yielded broken bones of a wide range of wild animals as well as others mostly domesticated such as horse, pig, celtic short-horned cattle and those of sheep and goats. Prof. Dawkins wrote; "The remains of the domestic dog were rather abundant, and the percentage of young puppies implies that, like other animals, they had been used for food".

Human bones were found in these caves also. The bones were in jumbled heaps, which indicated that they had been buried in the cave in a crouched position which was characteristic of neolithic interments. In one cave sixteen individuals were found. Earth and stones had to be removed before access could be gained. The stones had apparently been placed to close the entrance of the cave, so creating a sepulchre for the bodies.

Two further caves were investigated near Rhos Isa. These are known as the 'Rhos Ddigre caves' in literature, as this was the former name for this farm, changing in the late 1800s. The present Rhos Ddigre is the next farm but two up from Rhos Isa, this farm is also called Rhos Ucha. Confusion arises as both farms have had the same name at different times. Rhos Ddigre is a corruption of Bodigre/Buddugre (the spelling varies). Both farms were in the township of Buddugre yr Abbot (p. 24).

The remains found in the Rhos Ddigre caves were similar to those found in the other caves. In addition there were teeth of a bear, a stone celt ('axe') and eight fragments from two pots of the kind used as burial urns. The size of the pot which could be estimated was around nine inches across and four and a half inches high. A lower layer in one of the caves contained charcoal, flint flakes and fragments of pottery. This indicated that the cave had been used for human habitation before it had become a burial chamber.

The polished greenstone celt that was found in a Rhos Ddigre cave. It is 4¹/₂ inches long and about 2¹/₂ inches across the cutting edge. It is thought to have been made at the Graig Lwyd Axe factory at Penmaenmawr. It is apparently unused and may have been buried with the dead.
(Prof W. Boyd Dawkins)

The Bronze Age

This is the next age in our history, but now there is a wealth of evidence of the people who used to live here.

One peculiarity of this period was the method of burying the dead. A chieftain or other notable received somewhat different treatment from the others. He would be buried in a *cist faen* (stone chest). First the dead were cremated then buried. The ashes were gathered and placed in or under an urn which was placed in the cist under a large mound of soil (known as tumuli) or stones (known as cairns) - different types of barrow.

Cairns are to be found on the top of hills. There are five on Cyrn y Brain (Sir Watkin's Tower is built on one), two on Moel Garegog and one near Llyn Cyfynwy. Many of these are covered with heather and so inconspicuous.

The first tumulus to be excavated was that which was discovered in 1890 on Boncyn Porthmon (drover's bank) on the main road to Rhydtalog.

This tumulus has been much damaged and is difficult to distinguish from the surrounding countryside, but it is one of the heather-covered hummocks on the left between the track to Bodidris and the track to Llyn Cyfynwy. It is not always easy for the untrained eye to distinguish tumuli from other bumps in the landscape caused by quarrying, geological features and so on. The two of ours that are the easiest to see are on the Wrexham road. Leaving the village, there is one on the left a few hundred yards before Pen Dinas (not on the OS map); the second is also on the left near to the top of the bends past Casgan Ditw (this one is on the OS map).

Many of the tumuli are not shown on the OS maps, which can be dangerous for the tumulus. The south side of the tumulus near to the Plough public house was cut away during road widening as it was not shown on the map. It is now! When excavated this tumulus yielded four burials, each person being cremated before burial. There were two urn burials where an urn was inverted over the burnt bones, one pit burial and a fourth burial where there was cremation in a cist. The cist was 18 x 12 x 12 inches in size, constructed of stone slabs for the walls, floor and roof. These multiple burials indicate that there was a settled population in this area at around 500 BC.

Roman times

Unlike the Bronze Age people, the Romans left little visible evidence of their presence. Much of what follows is best regarded as enlightened guesswork. For example it is known that there were Roman settlements in Chester, near Wrexham and at Bala and it is logical to assume that roads ran between these, but without hard archaeological evidence it is not possible to be certain of the routes taken.

The Old Road is very straight. It is known locally as 'The Roman Road'. It is not always easy to distinguish a road that is called Roman because it is straight from one that is straight because it is Roman. Unless there are archaeological finds it is very difficult to date a road. Later, estate roads were sometimes built straight for the obvious reason that it is the shortest distance between two points. In the case of the Old Road it is possibly a Roman road, or runs parallel to the course of one. From Pen y Stryt the Roman road would have followed the same valley as the Wrexham road (A525) and then the Old Road past Pen Dinas until it meets the B5430, near the Four Crosses at Tan y Bwlch. Here it would have divided, one branch going to Ffrith, where it is known that silver, lead and other minerals were smelted and then on to Chester. The other branch would have followed the rest of the Old Road through Coedpoeth and then points south. The Wrexham side of Coedpoeth is known as *The Adwy* (gap or pass), so-called because there is a gap in Offa's Dyke there, so this may be an ancient route.

From Pen y Stryt the Roman Road continues up hill to Dafarn Dywyrch, west of the A5104 and the drovers' road (p. 30). It then ran between the A5104 and the minor road (also possibly a drovers' road) past Bodanwydog and Rhos Lydan. There is some archaeological evidence for this part of the route; AD73 has been suggested as a possible date for its construction. In a field just below the roundabout there is evidence of a small fort which is possibly Roman. This would have been in a strategic position at the heads of four valleys (as was Tomen y Rhodwydd, pp. 19-21) and overlooking fords across the River Alyn.

On the left of the modern A5104 to Chester, about a mile from Pen y Stryt, there is a straight track nearly a mile long that crosses a small valley. This is known as the Drovers' Road. The modern road hugs the hillside. Before roads were covered in tarmac, avoidance of boggy areas would have been important for travellers. This track is in rough alignment with the road from Rhydtalog through Treuddyn which is also very straight, so could have been part of a Roman route.

There are many straight roads in this area despite the hilly terrain. It is speculation to attribute these to any particular era. Llandegla is at a busy crossroads between the A525 and the A5104; it would seem likely that it has also been a busy crossroads for many centuries past.

St Tecla's Well

Not far from Llandegla Church and near to Mill Cottage is a field called *Gwern Tecla* and there by the river is a well which was once famous because of the superstitions associated with it. It is situated in thinly wooded boggy ground sloping down to the River Alyn. The Well itself is a chamber four feet by three feet and about a foot deep, the bottom being stone lined, surmounted by a well chamber about seven feet by five feet, the water coming from a spring beneath a large flat stone. Unfortunately the Well is now in great disrepair.

Saint Tecla's Well as it is today   *(Mrs Janet Robinson)*

In 1935 the Well was excavated by Alwyn Rees who found beneath the first layer of mud coins, pins and small fragments of pottery dating from the late eighteenth and early nineteenth centuries. Beneath this layer Mr Rees found dozens of white quartz pieces and also calcite varying in size from half an inch to four inches. The small pieces were water worn. White stones are often found in or around holy wells, although no-one in Llandegla remembers this custom.

In 1990 a small working party cleared much of the sludge that had collected in the well. They found that it had been carefully constructed of flat stones on two sides, with a third side formed of a single slab four feet long, which unfortunately had a large crack. The fourth side was badly damaged because two large alder trees had grown into it. There was a free stone by the well, inscribed :- AG0E:G or AGAT:G

It is believed that the Well has been there since Roman times and that it was dedicated to the worship of Aesculapius, the Roman god of healing. Later it was believed that it could cure epilepsy, known locally as *Clwyf Tecla* (Tecla's illness). The water has a very high calcium content. The drovers were said to have watered their cattle in the well to take advantage of the healing powers of the water to put their animals in good shape for the long journey ahead. During the severe drought of 1921 the well never failed to supply fresh water.

To be cured of epilepsy, the sufferer had to arrive at the Well after sunset on Friday, carrying a cockerel (if a man) or hen (if a woman). The bird was pricked with a pin which was thrown into the water (hence the pins found by Alwyn Rees). An offering of one groat (four pence) was made which was thrown into the water and the sufferer's face and feet washed in the Well.

The sufferer then had to carry the bird and circle the well three times, reciting the Lord's Prayer. After completing this task, the sufferer would go to the Church and circle the Church three times, again reciting the Lord's Prayer. The sufferer then entered the Church with the bird and slept under the altar, using the Bible as a pillow and the communion cloth as a blanket*. At daybreak the beak of the bird was placed in the sufferer's mouth who blew into it, thus transferring the disease. Before leaving, an offering of silver had to be placed into the poor box. The bird was left in the Church until the sufferer returned to the Well the following night to perform the same ritual. If the bird died the sufferer would be cured.

* This practice of sleeping under the altar would seem to have a very ancient origin. Sick Greeks and Romans would sleep within the precincts of a temple to Aesculapius to obtain a vision of the healing god who would reveal the remedy to the sleeper's illness in a dream. This was called *incubation*. At the time of Claudius, sick slaves would be left in the temple until recovery or death. If the former occurred, the slave would then be a free man - no doubt an inducement to become ill in the first place!

This custom came to an end around the middle of the eighteenth century for in 1749 the rural dean "gave strict charge to the parish clerk at his peril to discourage that superstitious practice, and to admit no one into the Church at night on that errand." Despite this, the custom persisted for some time. The last ceremony involving a chicken took place in 1813, but even as late as 1865 money was still being thrown into the Well by sufferers who wished to be cured of epilepsy.

Other Holy Wells

There are two other holy wells in the parish: St Collen's Well and St Garmon's Well. St Collen's Well is just inside the Llandegla parish boundary. It is about a hundred yards across the the slope from the first hawthorn bush on the road from the Ponderosa cafe to Pentre Dŵr. The road to Pentre Dŵr was the main road across the pass to Llangollen before the Horseshoe Pass was built in 1811. It was known as *Bwlch Uffern* (the Devil's Pass) because of its long steep slope.

The well is now much overgrown with rushes, but is still kept full with crystal clear water from a spring that issues from a rock to its left. Even in recent times the water has a reputation for curing warts. It is said that if the affected parts of the skin are bathed regularly in the water from the well, the warts will disappear in a few weeks.

(Phil Clark)

St Collen was a seventh century saint. When he was young he killed the pagan giantess Bras, a chieftain who was terrorising the neighbourhood and threatening the Christian Church. She lived at Graig Arthur, the next escarpment down from World's End. Though regarded as a hero, it was felt that Collen had used the wrong weapon as a Christian: the sword instead of saintliness. He was given a ceremonial absolution at the well which is still called after him. Later he returned to the area to found a Christian settlement, a *llan*, which still carries his name: Llangollen.

St Garmon's Well is sited in the field bounded by green railings by Saints' Crossing, where the Offa's Dyke Path crosses the B5431. It is in the hedgerow opposite. Unfortunately there is nothing to see but a few rocks in the side of a ditch: this historic site has virtually disappeared. St Garmon was an early Christian saint who wandered through North Wales, gathering converts and then founding settlements (*llan*). There are still nine churches dedicated to St Garmon, the nearest ones being at Llanarmon yn Iâl, Llanarmon Dyffryn Ceiriog and Maesgarmon (Mold). The water from St Garmon's Well would have been used for baptisms and other religious purposes.

Here the Offa's Dyke Path crosses the B5431 at Saints' Crossing. The acorn waymark is in the foreground. Saint Garmon's Well used to be in the hedgerow across the field behind the young tree on the left, but all traces have gone. The hedgerow on the right is in Llanarmon parish, that on the left in Llandegla parish. *(Janet Handley)*

The Roman heads

Above: The Roman heads that were found on Rhos Ddigre farm. *(Miss Eunice Francis)*

Left: Eunice Francis' grandmother at Rhos Ddigre farm before the heads were painted. *(Miss Eunice Francis)*

In about 1980 six stone heads were noticed at Rhos Ddigre Farm. It was estimated that they were carved between 100 BC and 200AD (although they could be pre-Roman). They may have been associated with St Tecla's Well, where the so-called Roman Stone, now used as a style, can be seen. The heads are not particularly unusual or valuable, but what is special about these is their number as they are usually found in ones or twos. If the association is valid, they are likely to have been put by the Well in thanks for a cure mediated by the Well. We are used to seeing bare stone antiquities, but these are painted. In Roman times these heads would also have been painted, so this is how they should be.

Tomen y Rhodwydd

Tomen y Rhodwydd, Llandegla's castle, is a well preserved earthwork of a motte and bailey castle. No buildings or superficial defences remain as they were made of wood, not stone. It is on private farm land, but can be seen from the road to Ruthin (A525) shortly after the junction with the Llanarmon road (B5431) and the old gate house, Garth Gate, which is now a cafe (pp. 27, 35).

This kind of castle was introduced by the Normans, though this one was built by the Welsh in 1149. The motte is a steep flat-topped mound, about 24 feet high and 22 yards across, surrounded by a ditch. The adjoining enclosure is the bailey, which covers about an acre, surrounded by a ditch and a dyke. This would have contained timber buildings used as living quarters, stables and so on, with a defensive wall around the edge.

This castle was built by Owain Gwynedd, Prince of Gwynedd. He had been steadily re-acquiring lands that had been previously lost to the Prince of Powys during his father's reign. Tomen y Rhodwydd was at the meeting point of four routes - Dyffryn Clwyd in the west towards Ruthin, Dyffryn Maelor in the east towards Wrexham (in the direction of the modern A525), the Alyn valley towards Mold in the north and towards Llangollen in the south. After its construction Owain Gwynedd was well protected from invasion and it also provided a base from which he could invade Powys if he desired.

However, six years later he was threatened by the forces of Henry II as well as those of Madog, prince of Powys. He was driven from Rhuddlan and realised that this new onslaught was too strong for him. He then agreed to give up the land between the rivers Clwyd and Dee, including Iâl, with Tomen y Rhodwydd. Subsequently Iorwerth Goch, brother of Madog, destroyed Tomen y Rhodwydd only eight years after it was built. As it was made of wood its destruction by fire would have been easy.

As the castle had no nearby settlement to give it a precise name when it was built, it was known as *Y Rhodwydd* which means 'earthworks of a camp or castle' (*tomen* means 'mound'). However on early maps it is labelled *Castell yr Adwy* - 'The Castle of the Pass'. This no doubt refers to its position between the end of the Clwydian Range and Llantysilio

Mountain. Both of these names are reflected in the names of nearby farms.

Castell y Rhodwydd in the evening sunlight. On the right is the A525 to Ruthin, the farm buildings at the top belong to Castell Farm. The road at the top is the old road to Ruthin via Graigfechan. *(Chris Musson, reproduced with permission from the Clwyd-Powys Archaeological Trust @ CPAT 84-32-25)*

The Welsh tribal system and its legacy

Every Welshman during the Dark and Middle Ages considered himself to be descended from a common ancestor. Those who claimed to be descended from this ancestor were grouped together in families, each group being a *llwyth* (tribe). The land that a tribe occupied was known as a *tref*. A number of trefs made up a *cwmwd* (comote) which was the administrative unit looked after by the *arglwydd* (lord).

Iâl was the name given to the cwmwd which consisted of what is known today as the parishes of Llanarmon, Llandegla, Bryneglwys and

Llantysilio. The seat of the Arglwydd was at Tomen y Faerdre in Llanarmon. He was maintained by his surrounding tribes of Bodidris, Chweleiriog, Bodanwydog and Trefydd Bychain, and about fourteen others further afield. The Cwmwd of Iâl was a branch of the Province of Powys and the residence of the Prince was at Castell Dinas Bran near Llangollen.

The four ancient tribe names mentioned still survive as names of farms (though Bodidris is now a hotel). As late as the 1879 map a broad swathe of land, roughly from the A542 in the west to the parish boundary in the east and north of Cyrn y Brain, was still being designated as Trefydd Bychain. One wonders for how many centuries that swathe of land has carried that name.

Townships, hundreds and counties

The Welsh *cwmwd* is equivalent to the English 'hundred'. The Hundred of Yale (Cwmwd yr Iâl) was an administrative unit within the county of Denbighshire. A *tref* is a 'township' on English maps, Trefydd Bychain being one of these townships. (The smallest unit was a *pentre*, originally referring to a dwelling, hence its use in farm names. In modern Welsh it means 'village'.) The hundreds and townships are secular in origin, the parish Christian, but collectively they formed a hierarchy - county, hundred, parish, township - which formed the basis of local administration from 1541 to 1972*. This apparently neat arrangement contained some anomalies due to the differing origins of its parts. For example the area around Bodidris and Llyn Cyfynwy which used to be in Llanarmon parish was in Flintshire, not Denbighshire as

* The Hundred of Yale finally lost its administrative significance in the first major reorganisation of the county boundaries in 1972. At that time Llandegla Parish was being administered by the Ruthin District Council within the old county of Denbighshire. The county of Clwyd was created through the amalgamation of Denbighshire, Wrexham and Flintshire. Within this, Llandegla Parish was part of Glyndŵr District Council. In 1996 the present unitary authority of Denbighshire was restored. Llandegla remains within the administrative area which covers the southern half of the old county of Denbighshire, much as Glyndŵr used to do.

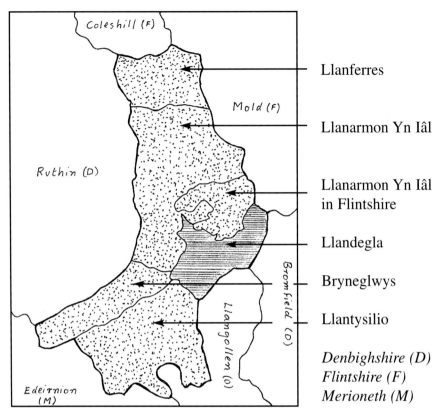

A map of the Hundred of Yale based on the 1883 OS map.

was the rest of this parish (see map on p. 6).

Unlike the surrounding hundreds, the Hundred of Yale seems to have kept its name and boundaries since early times. Above is an outline of the Hundred of Yale before 1920, showing its five constituent parishes and the neighbouring hundreds. The county borough of Wrexham Maelor now occupies much of the old Hundred of Bromfield.

The map opposite shows the ancient townships in the modern parish of Llandegla. The locations of the townships are approximate. By the time that precisely drawn maps became available the townships had lost much of their significance so their boundaries are not always shown, particularly in Denbighshire as it happens. There were just two townships in the old parish of Llandegla, Llan Township (Tre'r Llan) and Trefydd Bychain. For much of its length, the boundary between these two townships followed the stream, Yr Alun Bach, from the Raven Bridge until it met the old parish boundary at Tafarn y Gath (shown approximately on the map). Nearby was Llan Township detached (in Flintshire!), just over four and a half acres. The map of 1847 labels the parish north of the Old Road as being part of Llan Township (labelled ?Llan on the map below), but the map of 1879 does not. The positions of the townships on the lower left are much more uncertain. 'Buddugre' is spelt differently in different publications. Gwernol is the only free-standing township name to be found on modern maps.

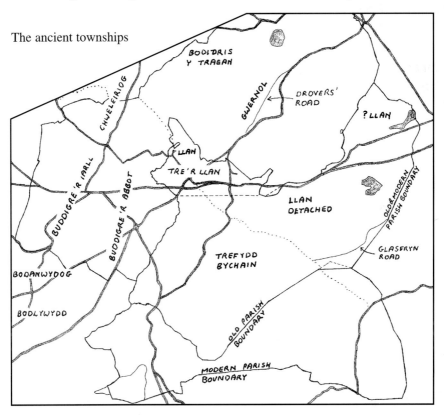

The ancient townships

BODIDRIS Y TRAEAN

CHWELEIRIOG

GWERNOL

DROVERS' ROAD

?LLAN

LLAN

TRE'R LLAN

BUDDIGRE 'R IARLL

BUDDIGRE 'R ABBOT

LLAN DETACHED

OLD & MODERN PARISH BOUNDARY

GLASFRYN ROAD

TREFYDD BYCHAIN

BODANWYDOG

BODLYWYDD

OLD PARISH BOUNDARY

MODERN PARISH BOUNDARY

The approximate locations of the ancient townships within the modern parish of Llandegla *(based on the 2000 Explorer Ordnance Survey map by permission of Ordnance Survey on behalf of the Controller of Her Majesty's Stationery Office, @ Crown Copyright MC 100033837)*

24

The parishes steadily became more important as administrative units rather than the townships, which lost their significance. This appears to have been due to the collection of tithes (see below), since the Church needed to know exactly from where the tithes were due. The township names were listed in the censuses of 1841-91, but have mostly disappeared from modern maps unless the names have persisted as names for farms.

Unlike the administrative units described above, the **manor** was about ownership. On the 1740 map an area of land is described thus: "Cefn dy in Bodigre'r Abbot *(sic)* Township in Llanarmon parish is part of the Manor of Valle Crucis" (p.8). The Valle Crucis lands, owned by the Hughes family of Coed Helen in Caernarfon then covered much of our local area including Llandegla village. Bodidris was not part of the Manor of Valle Crucis. On the map of 1667 it is shown to be of equal status to Llandegla. **Lordships**, like manors, were also about ownership. The Hundreds of Bromfield and Yale tended to be associated since they were granted together as a lordship to the Earl de Warrenne of Surrey by Edward the First. He also acquired Buddugre yr Iarll: the other part of this township Buddugre yr Abbot, was owned by Valle Crucis, hence the names.

The tithes system

Paying a tithe, which is one tenth of one's income, to the Church was generally accepted by the population in the Middle Ages. Subsequent to 1273, as a result of a controversy between Bishop Anian II and the Abbot of Valle Crucis Abbey, it was decided that all tithes raised in the Parish of Llandegla (which had been established around 1200) would be given to the incumbent. He was (and still is) known as the Rector, as this was the title for a clergyman who was in charge of a parish and who also received all of the tithes. A vicar only received part of the tithes. (Originally a vicar was deputy to a rector, but now this is also the title of a clergyman in charge of a parish.)

By the 1800's people were less willing to pay tithes, particularly in Wales where the growth of nonconformity and Methodist chapels caused hostility towards payment for the upkeep of the Church of England. A general decline in the prices for farmers' crops in the 1880's caused rural hardship, making the payment of tithes even more resented than before. This resentment led to the 'tithe war' which affected the Llandegla area between 1886 and 1891.

Farmers asked for a reduction in rent from their landlords and in tithes from the Church. Many received this but the Vicar of Llanarmon yn Iâl refused. Farmers refusing to pay their dues had their goods or animals 'distrained' - seized to be auctioned off to raise the money owed. No Welsh auctioneer would do this in Llanarmon, so one was brought in from Chester. He needed the protection of the Chief Constable of Denbighshire, an Inspector and sixty policemen. Bryniau Farm (now in the Parish of Llandegla, the boundaries being changed in the early 1920's) was the scene of one such auction described in the *Standard* of 24th August 1886:

"At Llanarmon yesterday a tithe distraint sale was announced to take place, and crowds of farmers attended. No auctioneer was present and the bailiffs had departed. Mr John Parry of Plas Llanarmon presided over a public meeting to protest against the action of the vicar. Two resolutions were passed condemning the vicar and pledging the farmers to use all constitutional means to obtain reduction of tithes. During the meeting a procession of lime-burners from Minera arrived brandishing staves. The crowd received them with cheers, but the leaders counselled peace and stolid opposition. A few minutes afterwards a cart arrived from Ruthin containing the vicar, solicitor's clerk and two bailiffs.

...The clerk walked through the crowd to the house of Mr Beech, one of the farmers distrained upon. As the clerk entered the farmyard one of the miners struck him with a staff and he fell.....

About 40 people ran after the cart and the two bailiffs. The driver set the horse to a gallop.... the animal shortly afterwards shied, throwing one of the bailiffs down. He was immediately set upon with staves, beaten about the head and left nearly for dead.

Stones were thrown at the others.....There is great excitement in the district and all work is suspended. It is feared that the disturbance may be renewed today. No police were present yesterday".

In 1896 the Royal Commission on Land in Wales made the farmers' grievances a matter of national concern. In 1920 the Church in Wales was disendowed and became separate from the Church of England. The last tithes known to be paid in Llandegla were by Accre Hall in about 1973. Despite these troubles, parishioners had a great loyalty to their parish. Even in the 20th century, before Llandegla parish was enlarged, people walked all the way from the southwest part of Llanarmon parish to their church instead of attending Llandegla Church which was much nearer.

When the past meets the present: Llandegla ghost stories

Llandegla has had a long history. Once in a while this history manifests itself long after it has passed. Such supernatural events can cause great alarm to the spectator. On the A5104, just outside Llandegla towards Chester, several travellers were badly scared by an apparition that loomed up in front of them on dark nights. Horses would become badly frightened and difficult to persuade to pass this spot. Sometime in the early twentieth century a skeleton was found by chance in a field beside the road, and then removed. Subsequently there were no further reports of apparitions. Until the early nineteenth century, criminals and those who had taken their own life could not be buried in consecrated ground: a roadside verge often sufficed instead. It is possible that this skeleton was that of one of these unfortunate individuals.

Another apparition was seen by some Canadian visitors to the Gate House (pp. 20, 35). Their description of the clothes worn by the person they had seen matched the standard dress of an eighteenth century toll-gate-keeper (also called a pikeman or pikey), even though they could not have known how he would have been dressed: corduroy breeches, white stockings, a white apron and a tall black glazed hat.

Only a few can claim to have seen a ghost firsthand, but some people appear to have a sensitivity to the supernatural, as the following two tales from Lou Thompson show:

"Asked by the landlord of the Hand Inn (before it closed) to help him out one evening, I was putting some change in the till in preparation for the night's business, when I sensed someone was standing behind me. I looked around to see a man standing at the bar. As it was only six p.m I pointed out to him that we would not be serving drinks till the proper opening time of seven pm. I turned to the till to close the drawer and walked from behind the bar to find that the man had disappeared. Though I was sure that the pub was locked and that I was the only person present in the building, I searched the pub from top to bottom and could find no one. Some weeks later I mentioned the incident to a lady who had lived in the village all her life, describing the man I had seen. She informed me that the person that I had seen was a previous owner of the pub and that he had died some years before.

One day in the summer of 1984 I took our King Charles spaniel for a walk heading towards the New Rectory. When we came to the big tree on the left hand side of the road opposite the New Rectory, the little dog refused to pass the tree and I was forced to turn around and go in another direction. Some months later when talking to a young lady who used to ride her horse along the same road, the conversation turned to a similar experience which she had of her horse refusing to pass that tree. Later on in the year, winter time in fact at about eight p.m, I tried the same walk again and on this occasion my dog would not even go as far as the tree: he appeared to be terrified. I looked farther up the road and I could see in the distance what appeared to be a very tall person dressed in what looked like a long white hooded gown on top of which there seemed to be a black apron. When the figure came close to me it looked like a monk who appeared to glide rather than walk. I could not see the face as the head was bowed, neither could I see the feet though the bottom of the gown seemed to be at least two inches off the ground. The little dog hid behind me trembling and stayed rooted to the spot until the figure had gone some distance from us. Eventually when I did get the dog to move we lost sight of whatever the figure was. A gentleman visiting the village told me that he had had a similar experience in exactly the same location, though later at night. I have seen this figure on several occasions since."

3. AS WE WERE: MORE RECENT HISTORY

The drovers

For many centuries there had been a trade in cattle between Wales and the Midlands and North of England. The cattle would be reared in upland areas and then driven to the lush pastures where they would be fattened for market. Welsh Blacks were ideal for this trade, being hardy cattle that quickly respond to favourable pastures. Drovers would be in a charge of a herd of cattle (a drove) as they travelled along traditional routes - the drove roads. From the time that the Romans left until the introduction of mail coaches, the drovers were the only regular long-distance travellers. Roads were generally atrocious until the building of the turnpikes in the 18th century. Because of the danger of robbery, or worse, travellers often joined a drove in order to travel safely.

Many of the drovers' roads have been lost, but between Raven Farm and Tŷn y Llidiart on the right looking uphill there is a long ditch which is an old drovers' road. The drovers preferred to drive the cattle over soft ground in order to reduce the wear on their feet. On a slope such as this the rain would have washed the churned soil away down hill. This would have left the road at the bottom of a steadily deepening cutting. Drovers from North West Wales would have used this road on the way to Llangollen. Other droves would have used the Old Road to go through Bersham to Wrexham and points south. Towards Chester there is a tradition that the drovers kept straight on after the Dolydd gate to meet the drovers' road (that which runs alongside the A5104). There is evidence of an old road, from maps and on the ground, along which they could have travelled (see map on p. 71). When a wall was being demolished at Pen y Bryn Farm some years ago various objects (unfortunately not recorded) were found hidden in the wall. Wrexham was rough in the old days and it was quite usual for drovers to hide objects of value in a wall for safety before making a visit.

The drovers had to take care, they could not afford to be cruel as they had to deliver their cattle in good condition. Cattle panic easily, especially

Welsh Blacks, so no drover could risk a sudden fright and scattering of cattle on a mountain pass. To drive these beasts over difficult country and such long distances was a job for a man with great skill. This care meant that they travelled only about ten miles each day. The drovers were not only extremely tough to withstand these arduous journeys, but were also literate and entrusted with money, letters and so on that needed to be sent long distances. However they were well paid. Because of the responsibility for this valuable cargo (both live and inanimate), and the occasional rogue, a system of licencing was introduced. A man could only obtain a licence for droving if he was over thirty, married and a householder. No hired servants were allowed. This meant that the men who drove the cattle for a large dealer had to do so under contract. Any man without a licence found droving was fined £5 (a lot of money in those days) and served a term of imprisonment. News also travelled via the drovers; this was the quickest way to make known locally events both at home and abroad.

Other animals also went along with the drove (but not pigs). At Raven Farm, which was once an inn, there is a hole in the stone wall where the geese had their feet tarred before the next part of their journey. This activity was also undertaken at Casgan Ditw and in the stable by the side of the Traveller's Rest.

Droving increased during the beginning of the nineteenth century. The Industrial Revolution was accompanied by a rapid increase in the urban population, which in turn led to an increase in the demand for food and therefore droving. However it was the industrial revolution that brought the railways, and so the demise of droving in about 1870. Railways had penetrated Wales to tap the mineral resources, but the cattle merchants were soon to take advantage of this new means of transport to send their stock by train. In addition at that time cattle plague and other diseases were causing indirect problems. Farmers were becoming very reluctant to provide overnight accommodation for a drove in case the cattle would carry disease to that farm.

The drovers grazed their cattle on the Dolydd ('meadows'), a field near the River Alyn on the road to Bodidris. There was a smithy on the village hill (p. 46), another by the first Dolydd Gate (by the cattle grid) and a third at Pen Rhos. The village smithy is now a garage and workshop. That at Pen Rhos has been demolished in recent times. The smithy by the first Dolydd Gate is not on the 1879 OS map, but there used to be a single storey cottage in the widened part of the road just before the cattle grid, which was in occupation about sixty years ago. It is likely that this was the old smithy. There is nothing to be seen there now, but the remains of the buildings used to be known as 'Little Llandegla'. There are two old stone gate posts built into the wall just on the other side of the cattle grid which are possibly the original Dolydd Gate posts. The position of the second Dolydd Gate is conjectural (see map on p. 6). At this point there is a modern bridge over the ancient water course. It was also where the old parish and old county boundaries used to run along the ancient water course, and possibly the original crossing of Afon y Dolydd (p. 118). Just beyond the bridge there is a double row of trees (now home to a farm building), typical of an old road.

Evidence that Llandegla was an important stopping point for the drovers is the number of pubs that were once in the area (pp. 89-101) and the fact that there were four fairs a year. The lead men would have slept in the pubs with the drovers sleeping in the hedgerows. The pubs were often marked by three Scots pines which could be seen from a long way away. Until very recently there were three pines behind the village shop which used to be the Blue Bell Inn.

In the heyday of droving Llandegla had sixteen pubs. It was quite usual in those days for a farm to be attached to a pub to provide additional living for the landlord, or for the farmer's wife to use the pub to supplement the farm income. Other businesses were also carried out - there was a horse dealer and a butcher at the Plough at different times, and there used to be a cattle market by the Crown Hotel. The Crown Hotel still owns a field. However, with the decline of droving, all these pubs could no longer be supported. Only two are still in use as pubs, the Crown Hotel and the Plough: most of the rest are private houses or farms.

Tai unnos

Tai unnos at Tafarn y Gâth   *(Mr Tegla Jones)*

The above photograph shows two cottages *(tai unnos)* at Tafarn y Gâth bridge on the A525, about 300 yards from Tafarn y Gâth towards Wrexham. The slopes of Cyrn y Brain are on the right, now covered by Llandegla Forest. There is a lay-by at the site of these cottages. This is the only photograph which has come to light showing this kind of building in Llandegla. Two cottages at Tafarn y Gâth are listed in the 1861 census, a lead miner living in one and a lime burner in the other. It is quite possible that this entry refers to these two cottages.

Cottages were not often supplied by employers for their employees on the farm or in the quarry, so they built their own on a convenient piece of land. The tradition was that if a cottage was built in one day *(tŷ unnos)* during the hours of darkness and had smoke coming from the chimney the following morning, the builder would then become the owner of the cottage and the land around it as far from the door as he could throw an axe. Though usually employed elsewhere, the cottagers would run a smallholding *(tyddyn* - the word often forms part of a place name) on a few acres around the cottage. George Borrow *(Wild Wales)* passed such a building in 1854 and his guide described it thus to him;

"That is a house, sir, built yn yr hen dull in the old fashion, of earth, flags and wattles in one night. It was the custom of old when a house was to be built for the people to assemble, and to build it in one night of common materials, close to hand. The

custom is not quite dead. I was at the building of this one myself, and a merry building it was. The cwrw da passed quickly about among the builders, I assure you".

It is likely that the original Dafarn Dywyrch, a "turf inn", would have been similarly built. (p. 99)

Toll roads through Llandegla

By the seventeenth century, the country was coming to realise that the deplorable condition of the roads was inhibiting trade. As a consequence a series of acts was enacted in Parliament enabling groups of people, the turnpike trustees, to levy tolls for the improvement of the roads. Like other businesses, some succeeded, some did not and some people made a lot of money out of the system. The local turnpike trust existed between 1740 and 1859. Sometimes with justification people began to feel that the tolls were not all being used on the roads, and for poor people the tolls were particularly onerous. Eventually this system became so unpopular that there were riots, the Rebecca riots, with the toll gates being destroyed. The toll gates were just one of the social and economic

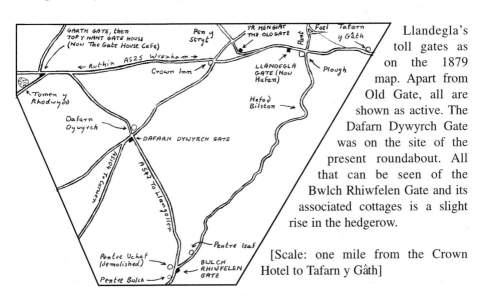

Llandegla's toll gates as on the 1879 map. Apart from Old Gate, all are shown as active. The Dafarn Dywyrch Gate was on the site of the present roundabout. All that can be seen of the Bwlch Rhiwfelen Gate and its associated cottages is a slight rise in the hedgerow.

[Scale: one mile from the Crown Hotel to Tafarn y Gâth]

pressures of the time, exacerbated by poor harvests, but they formed an obvious target for the protests. In response to the Rebecca riots a commission was appointed in 1843 which proposed the establishment of a Highways Board in each Welsh county. This became law in the following year. The turnpikes were eventually taken over by the Highway Boards.

The turnpike between Ruthin and Wrexham passed through Llandegla. In addition a turnpike left Llandegla for Llangollen. Later, a turnpike was built towards Chester via Rhydtalog. No record of a toll gate for this turnpike in Llandegla parish has been found, but there was a tollgate on the present A5104 where the Treuddyn turn forks left.

Originally there were five toll gates in Llandegla. One in the west towards Ruthin was the Garth Gate, now the Gate House Cafe. A second, the Bwlch Rhiwfelen Gate, now demolished, was opposite the entrance

The Garth Gate at the junction of the A525 to Ruthin (in the foreground) and the B5431 to Llanarmon, but also the original road to Ruthin via Graigfechan. The B5431 passes from the right of the photograph behind Garth Gate. The building has been much altered, the single storey section on the right is probably the only original feature left. It is now the Gate House Cafe, which is reputed to be haunted. George Borrow passed this way in 1854. He refers to the Nant y Garth as the 'New Road'. There was a gate across this, as well as the 'Old Road' to Ruthin via Graigfechan, down which he travelled. *(Mrs Janet Robinson)*

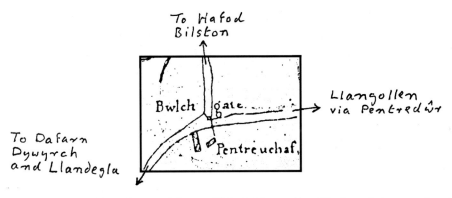

The Bwlch Rhiwfelen Gate and Pentre Uchaf (*Upper Dwelling*), and the associated cottages, taken from the Enclosure map thought to be 1847. These buildings have all disappeared, though the remains of the cottages have been seen within living memory. In contrast, the first farm on the Hafod Bilston road, Pentre Isaf (*Lower Dwelling*), is still very much a working farm. The Bwlch Rhiwfelen Gate and Pentre Uchaf are not shown on the 1912 OS map, though the building for the Dafarn Dywyrch Gate is still shown.

to the road to Pentre Isaf and Hafod Bilston, on the right of the A542 approaching the Horseshoe Pass. A third was on the site of the existing roundabout opposite Dafarn Dywyrch Farm. This gate was across the Corwen road. Tolls for Llangollen and Hafod Bilston would have been collected by the Bwlch Rhiwfelen Gate, which was across both roads at their junction.

The situation as regards the two toll gates on the Wrexham road is more enigmatic. The map of 1830 shows a toll gate on Old Gate Lane. On a map of 1878 this is shown as 'the Old Gate'. A few hundred yards from the Plough Inn, Llandegla Gate is shown on this map. This is the private house now known as *Hafan*. The first record for this house is in 1704 when it "became a toll house", so this building was already in existence by then. It is mentioned in 1823 when further powers were given to the turnpike trust, so it was active then. In 1879 it was sold to the tollcollector, Thomas Jones, for £91. This presumably was when the Road Board was taking over the turnpike. By 1912 it was known as Voel View, but it has also been known as Heather Brae, Haroline and Rose Cottage before its present name for thirty-one years, Hafan.

Llandegla Gate, now Hafan. This has been rebuilt but the stone gateposts appear to be original. They are typical toll gate posts. These posts would have been on each side of the road when the gate was in use *(Mrs Janet Robinson)*

The question that arises is: were both toll gates active at the same time, or was the Llandegla Gate not operating for a few years around 1830? This is not known at present, the Llandegla Gate is not shown on the 1830 map. The toll house on Old Gate Lane was converted into three cottages - *Yr Hen Giât*. The lane used to be very narrow at that point and the cottages were in a poor state so they were demolished when the road was widened. No trace can now be seen. The Gate may have been active for only a short time but its legacy is in the name of the lane that it crossed.

Below: The pattern of roads before the new road was constructed *(redrawn by Phil Clark from an Enclosure map, thought to be 1830)*

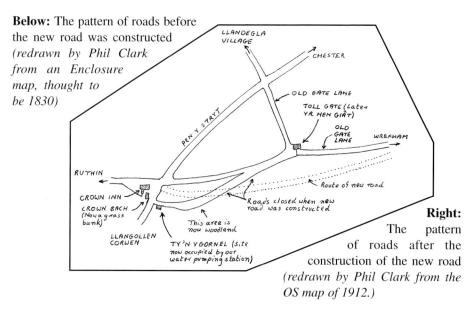

Right: The pattern of roads after the construction of the new road *(redrawn by Phil Clark from the OS map of 1912.)*

Old Gate, Llandegla.

Yr Hen Giât in 1910. These are the three cottages that were made from the old toll house. By the early 1960's they were in a bad state. In 1965 a demolition or closing order was served on the owners (who were not local) as No. 2 was "unfit for human habitation and is not capable of being made fit at a reasonable cost." Subsequently they were demolished and the road widened. The cottage in the middle, partly hidden by the gable end of Garden Cottage, is Bryn Tirion where Tegla Davies (p.190) was born. The cottage on the left is Brynhyfryd, the home of the Reverend Samuel Evans (p.187). Old Gate Lane swings right behind Yr Hen Giât towards Llandegla village. The track that leaves the lane to the left to pass in front of Bryn Hyfryd is the path of the original road to the Crown crossroads. *(Reproduced with permission from Denbighshire Record Office, Ruthin)*

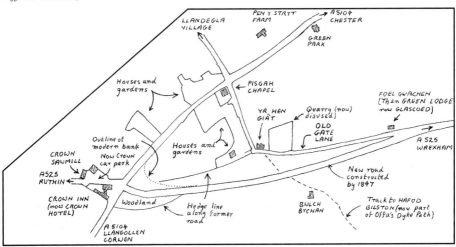

This stone was found as a doorstep in the Crown Sawmill. It reads, "Toll for Bromfield and Yale". Bromfield is now basically the county borough of Wrexham. It is uncertain from which toll house it came. It has now been carefully built into a wall during the restoration of the sawmill (p.86). *(Mrs Janet Robinson)*

Nineteenth century Llandegla

Census returns are made available to the general public one hundred years after the census has been taken. For Llandegla the census returns for 1841 until 1891 are available for reference. Interestingly, the township names are still listed.

An entry in the 1841 census lists a family of cattle drovers, headed by John Jones, who lived at Pentre Isaf. By 1891 droving had all but come to an end and the cattle drover who lived in Foel must have been the last of his kind. Some other industries have also disappeared: the lead mines (p.132) and quarries have closed. Limestone is no longer burnt. Our native limestone is too hard and insoluble to be used on the fields and had to be converted into quicklime. This is very unpleasant stuff to handle (worse than cement). Limestone and charcoal were put into a kiln and fired to about 1,000 degrees centigrade. After being taken out of the kiln, the quicklime was put into heaps and water was poured over it. The heap became a hot steaming mass. When the resulting slaked lime had cooled it could be spread on the fields to reduce the acidity of the soil. Slaked lime was also used to make lime mortar for building and for whitewash. There were quite a number of lime kilns dotted around

Llandegla Parish where limestone was easily accessible. Lime kilns were built by a quarry as near as possible to where the lime was to be used because of the difficulty of transport. It now comes by lorry: local lime burners have long since gone.

In each census several shoemakers are listed which seems rather a lot for a small village. As well as farming, other trades such as quarrying, lead mining and lime burning would have taken a heavy toll of footwear. Also, for ordinary people in those days walking was the only means of transport until public transport became available and affordable in the twentieth century. This necessity for walking had other effects apart from the need for a supply of shoes. It was not unusual for people to spend their entire life in one village or nearby. Even in 1891 most inhabitants were born locally or in Llanarmon yn Iâl, though people from nearby parishes of Llanfair Dyffryn Clwyd and Bryneglwys are also recorded.

A number of people are listed as paupers in the censuses. These were people who had no means of earning a living and relied on poor law relief. The Poor Law of 1601 levied a tax on all occupiers of property to provide for the poor: this was the origin of the rating system as we know it today. Its aim was to provide materials for work for the able bodied and relief for the disabled and incapacitated. A newcomer who was likely to be a charge on the parish could be sent back to his native parish. From 1815 workhouses were built to house people who could not earn their own living. Able bodied paupers were expected to go to the workhouse, though those in Llandegla appeared to be living in their own homes. Conditions in the workhouse were harsh to discourage people from "going to the parish" and keep costs down. There was a workhouse in Ruthin on the present site of Ruthin Hospital.

The fear of having to go to the workhouse induced many skilled workers to form friendly societies to cushion the effects of sickness and unemployment. In 1834 there was a much needed shake-up of the administration. Several parishes were combined together to form Poor Law Unions, the boundaries of which are shown on maps of the time and also on the ground (p.130). This made it easy to identify which Union was responsible for whom. In Llandegla the Union Friendly Society was formed in 1834, the Llandegla Female Friendly Society in 1840 (pp.194-197). (Even in the 1930's a pauper could obtain 'tickets', each of which was worth four pence, which would buy four ounces of bread and two ounces of cheese.)

In the 1891 census, youths between fourteen and fifteen make up the largest group. There were more children than people aged fifty or more. The majority spoke Welsh, a small number spoke English only and about twenty percent of villagers spoke both languages. Though the parish was much smaller then than today, this list taken from the 1891 census shows how many different trades there were in such a small village:

Agricultural labourer	Miller
Blacksmith	Minister
Boot and shoe dealer	Parish Clerk
Butcher	Pauper
Butter and cheese dealer	Police Officer
Carpenter	Professor of Music *(from Scotland!)*
Carter	Publican
Cattle dealer	Quarry agent
Cattle drover	Rector
Dressmaker	School master
Domestic servant	School mistress
Draper	Scholar *(school pupil)*
Farm bailiff	Shepherd
Farmer	Shoemaker
General labourer	Slate quarry agent
Grocer	Slate worker
Groom	Slater
Highway labourer	Soldier
Housekeeper	Tailor
Innkeeper	Veterinary surgeon
Lead miner	Wheelwright
Lime quarryman	Water trench keeper *(for the new Pen Dinas leat?)*

Another source of information is the Flintshire and Denbighshire Postal

Directory for 1886, an early "Yellow Pages". It gives a brief description of each village and town and then a list of officers and businesses. It describes Llandegla thus: *"...the soil here is of good quality, but the climate cold on account if its proximity to the mountains"*. One also gains the impression that Pen y Stryt was an active village in its own right in earlier times, in contrast to today when it is mostly residential. Mentioned in the Directory are:

Mr Davies, farmer, Accre Farm.
Edward Edwards, grocer and sub-postmaster, Post Office *(letters were dispatched and received from Mold daily)*.
Rev Samuel Evans, "Independent Chapel" *(of Pisgah Chapel. He must have been retired, or nearly so by then)*.
Daniel Jones, farmer, Pen y Bryn.
Ellis Jones, grocer, Pen y Stryt.
Mrs Jones, "lic. vict.", The Hand.
Robert Jones, farmer and miller, The Mill. *(presumably St Thomas Mill)*.
Thomas Jones, castrator and farmer, Tŷ'n y Llidiart.
William Jones, (Ehedydd Iâl), farmer, Tafarn y Gâth
Rev J Owen, "Vicar, The Vicarage" *(presumably the Old Rectory)*.
Robert Parry, draper and grocer, Pen y Stryt.

Robert Roberts y Wyau (with the eggs), Bethan Roberts (midwife) on the right.

(Mr W. Owen)

42

Now it is so easy to travel, the local tradesmen that used to supply the needs of the village are no longer, such as the besom maker, blacksmith, tailor, miller, cooper (in Nant y Cwm in 1851, perhaps less isolated then when the quarries were active), gate keeper (we pay road tax now instead) and washerwoman. Entertainment then was local and home made. It centred around the church, chapels and pubs. Since most inhabitants had lived in the same village for all their lives, they knew each other very well. All this induced a prolific social life which the present generation looks back on with nostalgia.

Two nineteenth century lives: *(Mr Tegla Jones)*

Ehedydd Iâl (1815 - 1899), a notable hymn writer and bard, was born William Jones in Derwen (near Llanelidan), son of a farm worker. William did not receive any formal education. When he was seventeen he obtained a copy of a Welsh Grammar by Robert Davies and with the help of friends he learnt to read and write. He wrote many poems and had them published in a book called *Blodau Iâl*.

After working on a farm in Gwyddelwern for eight years he moved to Rhydmarchogion, Llanelidan, as a farm bailiff to Mrs Davies. It was there that he wrote his famous hymn *"Er nad yw 'nghnawd ond gwellt"*, when he was asked by Mrs Davies to write a poem to console Ruth, her daughter, who was seriously ill. He moved to Green Park for a short time, then had a job as a miller in Minera. He was then offered the tenancy of Tafarn y Gâth (p.93). He did not enjoy being an inn keeper and after eight years was able to give up that work. He was reputed to have a quick wit and ready repartee, and was popular as a compere at concerts and eisteddfod. In the poem he says:

> *"although my skin be straw*
> *and all my bones but clay*
> *I sing through the lightning*
> *God forgave me my faults*
> *The rock of ages is under my feet,*
> *And the lightning is put out by the blood."*

Ehedydd Iâl (1815 - 1899). This photograph, donated by the late Mrs Alan Jones, hangs in the committee room of the Memorial Hall.

Left: Rhewl Glyn Rhys before 1912

Below: Daniel Roberts with his youngest son, Benjamin

(Mr Tegla Jones)

Daniel Roberts (18.. - 18..), Tegla Jones' great-grandfather, was the village tailor. He lived at Rhewl Glyn Rhys near the Crown Hotel. He had eight children. One son, Thomas, became the village blacksmith, Mrs Eileen Clark's grandfather. Two other sons, Robert and Benjamin, followed him as tailors. They would visit farms making clothes as ordered or villagers would bring their orders to the house. According to their records a pair of trousers would cost three shillings (about £5 today) and a vest one shilling and six pence. The tailoring came to an end in the early 1930's.

Llandegla life in the early twentieth century

There used to be a great variety of trades in Llandegla serving the needs of the farms and households. This self-reliance was essential when roads were poor making transport slow and difficult. Viewing village life today, it is difficult to comprehend the immense change that has occurred in such a short period of time. A recurrent theme is the pervading influence of the Bodidris estate on village life, especially during the years of the benevolent influence of Captain and Mrs Dewhurst.

The following memories of the village blacksmith (Daniel Roberts' grandson) are from Mrs Eileen Clarke who is now in her seventies:

"The smithy was owned by the Roberts family. My father Robert Hugh Roberts (Bob) took over the smithy when his father Thomas died at fifty-six years. He was a master blacksmith who had done his apprenticeship at Cammel Lairds shipyard and had hoped to continue there for many more years. But things had deteriorated, accounts for materials were unpaid due to my grandfather's illness and bills for work done were also not being paid. It was very difficult for my father. The only solution was to sell the smithy to the estate. This was done, at Captain Dewhurst's sug-

gestion. My father was then employed working three days in the smithy and three on the estate.

I cannot tell the real story without including Walter Evans, Mrs Flora Edwards' father. They worked together on many things. My earliest memory of the Smithy is sitting on a sack in the forge itself watching how the horse shoes were made. I must have been three or four years old. They were heated, shaped, cooled and then fitted on the hooves, the procedure went on until they were a perfect fit. There were no bought shoes

Robert Hugh Roberts at the door of the Smithy, caught at work with a hammer in one hand and tongs with a horseshoe in the other! *(Mrs Eileen Clarke) then. Chains, hinges, latches, hoops for wheels, repairs for all manner of farm machinery were made. This is where Walter came in. He made all the wooden parts for carts, gates, handles for ploughs (horse drawn then), doors, everything that was needed on the estate. They worked in partnership and fortunately were good friends.*

An exciting day for us children was hooping day. The wheels were brought to the forge, put on a stand outside, hoops heated almost white hot, skilfully put on the wheels and hosed down with gallons of water to cool. Steam rose and the water flooded down the village. I could never understand why the wheels did not burn: I cannot recall any that did.

My father made flue irons. It was a joke in our house that we were the only family without a proper kitchen poker (a case of the cobblers' children). He loved fashioning all sorts of metals. His favourite was brass: we had a beautiful fender with all the

fireirons in the parlour, which I had to polish when I got older. When the brass things were made they had to be rubbed down with varying degrees of sandpaper until the colour came through. It took patience and a very long time. He made brass horse shoes, these were given as wedding presents mounted on a polished wood base (Walter again)."

Walter Evans at the back of what is now Rose Cottage. He worked upstairs as joiner for the Bodidris estate. He also helped his neighbour Robert Edmund Jones, the undertaker. Mr Jones made coffins by candlelight in the shed behind Walter Evans. *(Mrs Flora Edwards)*

The village in 1929. The two children are Dennis Roberts (son of Robert Hugh Roberts and great grandson of Daniel Roberts) and Brenda Bromige, whose father took the photograph. The motorbike belonged to the district nurse who used to live in the end cottage of the village cottages: she did her rounds on it. The farm building on the right belonged to Bodawen. *(Mrs Eileen Clarke)*

Mrs Clarke continues:

> *"The place now known as the Sawmill was called the Stores where all things wooden were made by Walter. All the wood came off the Estate, was sawn up as floor boards etc, dried and then used. All the logs needed for Bodidris fires were sawn there."*

Walter Evans, son of John Evans, the village postman, was the joiner for the Bodidris estate. He and his wife Ethel had two daughters, Flora and Dorothy. They lived in Queens Cottage. Flora, born in 1917, worked for a time as a kitchen maid at Bodidris where she learnt, among other things, to dress game. She married Howell Edwards from Bwlchgwyn in June 1942 and went to live at No 1, Village Cottages, which was rented from the Dewhursts. On Boxing Day 1942, her sister Dorothy married James Hindley.

John Evans, the village postman, and his wife, who lived at Green Lodge, now Glascoed. They were the parents of Walter Evans. *(Mrs Flora Edwards)*

The link with Bodidris runs through Jim Hindley's life also. Born on 22nd November 1914 in Rhydtalog, he was the eldest son of George and Elizabeth Hindley, with an older sister, Mary, and a younger brother, Harry. His father was a gamekeeper on the local estate (his brother Harry followed in his father's footsteps to become the head keeper). Jim moved to Llandegla in 1920 when his father was made head gamekeeper on the Bodidris Estate for the Dewhurst family. The family home was Plas yn Coed.

As a child, Jim attended the local school in Llandegla. After leaving school he too became an apprentice gamekeeper on a large estate in Somerset. In the 1930's he had a change of careers to become a steel erector and steeplejack, working on a number of large chimney stacks of the coal-fired power stations around Britain, including one which can still be seen today in Ferrybridge, Yorkshire. He continued this career throughout the war years. During the short periods when he returned home to Llandegla he would help his father and father-in-law, who were members of the local Home Guard, to light fires around the top of Moel

Garegog and the Duck Pool. This was an area he knew well from his childhood days, when he would go around the mountains helping his father with his gamekeeper duties. The purpose of these fires was to divert the German planes from bombing Liverpool and drop their bombs on the mountain instead. This was somewhat successful, with a number of bombs being dropped on the mountains, it is reputed that a number of unexploded bombs are still in the peat bogs on those mountains (pp.64-65).

Jim and Dorothy had two sons, Clive born in 1944 and Colin born in 1946. In 1948 he and his family moved into number 4 Council Houses, (now known as 4 Maes Teg), which was one of the new houses built in Llandegla after the end of the war. Later that year Jim had a serious accident while working in a power station in Sheffield, which resulted in him losing part of his left arm. This ended his career as a steeplejack. Following his recovery from his injuries, Jim went to work for Clifford Hughes, a civil engineering contractor in Ruthin. While with this company he worked on a number of large engineering projects in and around the North Wales area, including the building of the original retaining walls of the A55, which can be still seen by Penmaenmawr. In the mid fifties, after being made redundant by the civil engineering company he had another change in career, working for the Egg Packing Station in Wrexham. This firm collected the eggs from the local farms around Wrexham, including Llandegla.

When this closed in the late fifties, he went to work with his brother-in-law, Howell Edwards, for Wrexham Sawmills in Rivulet Road, Wrexham. In the early sixties he became the foreman in charge of the Crown Sawmill in Llandegla. In this role he became well known to all the farmers and traders around the area and many of the locals. He also became well known to people moving into the Llandegla area, supplying them with timber and fencing materials and advising them on the use of wood and materials for their DIY activities. He remained at the sawmills as the manager until his retirement at the age of sixty-seven.

For thirty years before his death in 1985 he was an active member of a number of committees and helped to run events in the village, including the re-development of the village hall and introduction of the village fete. In the 1950's he became treasurer of the snooker club in the village hall, snooker being one of his main hobbies. He would get the tables erected and ironed ready for the club members, using the old irons which were heated on the coal stoves in the hall before electricity came to the village. In the late sixties he was elected to the local parish council. He became an active member of the council: being well known throughout the region, he would use his contacts to get help to solve problems for the village. After retiring he continued to work for the community, when he became the treasurer of the Darby and Joan Club.

Flora Edwards, his sister-in-law, lived in Llandegla all her life. She had a long and loyal friendship with Dilys Davies (pp.189, 212), starting when the Davies came to live at No 2, Village Cottages. (Dilys' father had also worked at the estate saw mill at the beginning of the 1940's.) The two friends walked many miles together, collecting for Poppy Day and charities such as "Fallen Women" (for the diocese of St Asaph): their visits around the farms were a regular event and an opportunity for friendly chats and the exchange of news. Flora died on

August 16th 1998 and Dilys in March 1999: sadly they did not live to see the final production of this book towards which they made a significant contribution.

Flora (left) and Dilys (right) on the occasion of Flora's eightieth birthday, 1997. *(Haydn Edwards)*

51

Another village family whose lives were interwoven with the Bodidris estate were the Jones of Ffynnon Wen. The farm of Ffynnon Wen was part of the Bodidris estate. William Jones was a farmer at the dawn of the twentieth century. His wife was Tegla Davies' aunt. They had four children: William Lloyd, Idris, Olive, and Doris. William Lloyd Jones became an estate maintenance worker, working alongside Walter Evans. His wife Minnie (nee Sandbach) looked after the linen at Bodidris. Idris worked there before moving on, as did Doris for a short time (before marrying Hugh Hughes from Anglesey) though she didn't much like the work. Olive's husband was John Bellis from Leeswood, the forestry manager for the estate. William's grandson, Ken Bellis, and his wife now live on the land which he bought at the break-up of the estate in 1978 which includes all the land which used to be Ffynnon Wen.

William Jones in 1920 at Ffynnon Wen. *(Mr & Mrs. K. Bellis)*

Some of the Bodidris estate workers in 1915. Some had farm smallholdings as well as helping with work on the estate.

Top, from left to right: William Jones, Tomen yr Adwy; Thomas Jones, slaterer, plasterer and sexton of the Church (Betty Forster's grandfather); Thomas Hughes, Bryn Hyfryd; John Hughes, Dafarn Dywyrch; William Lloyd Jones, Ffynnon Wen, apprentice with Thomas Jones.
Bottom, from left to right: John Jones, Tŷ Coch, stone mason and grate setter; Evan Jones, Tan y Fron; William Ellis, nephew of the ladies at Glan yr Afon.
(Mrs Betty Forster)

A wedding party in the Memorial Hall, August 15th 1931: Olive Jones; Ted Hughes (the bridegroom's brother); Hugh Hughes (the bridegroom); Doris Hughes nee Jones (the bride); William Lloyd Jones; Minnie Jones nee Sandbach. *(Mr & Mrs K Bellis)*

Four generations outside Ffynnon Wen, about 1936: Mrs William Jones aged sixty-two, her mother Mrs Davies aged eighty-six, Mrs Doris Hughes (nee Jones) aged twenty-seven and baby Alun aged just two years. Doris is now ninety-four and still going strong!
(Mr & Mrs K Bellis)

More estate workers. In the background is the saw bench with the circular saw, originally powered by steam. **From left to right:** Robert Roberts, blacksmith, Bodawen (Mrs Eileen Clarke's father); Will Evans, Lletty; Mr Edwards, Bodanwedog; Mr Davies from Bryneglwys; Idris Jones, Ffynnon Wen. *(Mrs Flora Edwards)*

4. THE WAR YEARS

War memorials

The legacy of the Great War was traumatic: seven men lost their lives during the conflict. For this village, which then had a small and declining population, it was a disaster to have lost so many active young men in such a short space of time. It was natural that permanent memorials would soon be set up in their memory: the Memorial Hall with a Memorial Plaque and the Cenotaph.

The Memorial Hall used to be a Wesleyan Chapel (pp.189-190), which closed in 1914 due to a dwindling congregation. Mrs Dewhurst of Bodidris bought the Chapel, restored it, and later gave it to the village. It was opened as the Llandegla War Memorial Hall on 17th June 1918 by the Lord Bishop of St Asaph. A plaque listing those that fell in the Great War was fixed to a wall in the Hall. Names were added to these after the Second World War and a window in the Parish Church was also dedicated.

The school record book records that on the 11th November 1919 on the first anniversary of the Armistice, in accordance with the King's appeal, silence was observed at 11.00 am, the Lord's Prayer repeated and the National Anthem sung. A Remembrance Service is still held on the Sunday nearest to the 11th November near to the Cenotaph, or in the Memorial Hall if the weather is bad. A member of the community selected by the Community Council lays a wreath and other organisations or relatives lay wreaths.

The Armistice service in the Memorial Hall in 1998.
(Mrs Jean Wilkinson)

Ash John	Rhosddigre	Private	
Bloor, John	Church Terrace	Private	K.I.A. 1918
Cammock, Alexander	Bodidris	Private	K.I.A.
Davies Benjamin	Bryndwr	Private	
Davies, David	Bryndwr	Private	
Davies, William Hughes	Bryndwr	Private	K.I.A.1916
Davies, Robert Thomas	Pen y Stryt	Private	
Davies Owen, H.	Tegla Cottage	Private	
Dawson, Alfred	Bodidris	Private	
Dewhurst, G. Powis	Bodidris	Capt	
Evans, John	Pen Lan	Private	
Evans, Meredith	Lletty	Private	
Evans, Ifor Alan	Green Lodge	Private	
Evans, John Parry	Green Lodge	Private	
Evans, Goronwy C.	Green Lodge	Private	
Edwards, Evan	Hand Inn	Gnr	K.I.A.1918
Ellis, Ed Vaughan	Glanrafon	Private	
Ellis, Thomas J.	Tŷ Uchaf	Private	
Griffiths, H.G.	Castell	Sgt	
Hughes, David	Brynhyfryd	Private	
Harrison, E.S,	Plough	D.R.	
Harrison, Herbert	Bwlchbychan	Private	
Hindley, George	Rhydtalog	Sgt Major	
Hope, Gordon	Bodelwyddan	Private	
Hope, Henry Noel	Bodelwyddan	Private	
Jones, Daniel	Tanygraig	Private	
Jones, Ellis	Tanyfoel	Private	
Jones, Hugh	Tanyfoel	Private	
Jones, Llewelyn	Rose Cottage	Private	
Jones, John Hugh	Bryman	Private	
Jones, Joseph	Graig	Private	
Jones, Trevor	Erwfawr	Private	
Jones, Evans	Tan y Fron	Sgt	
Jones, John R.	Casgan Ditw	Private	
Lamont Thomas	Bodidris	Private	
Morris, Humphrey	Bryniau	Private	
Moss Samuel	Accre	Sec Lieut	
Owens, John O.	Rhos Cottage	Private	
Parry, John	Old Gate	Private	K.I.A.1918
Robson, Peter	Maesmaelor	Private	
Robson, Mathew	Maesmaelor	Private	
Roberts, John Edward	Pen y Stryt	Lance Cpl	
Roberts, R.T.	Graig	Private	
Rhone, Fred	Bodidris	Private	
Smith, Sydney	Bodidris	Private	
Thomas, Edward	Tanyfron	Sgt	
Thomas, Richard	Tanycreigiau	Sgt	
Williams, Joseph	Garth Gate	Sgt	
Parry, Thomas	Fronhaul	Private	

The following were killed in the Second World War 1939-45
Jones, Glyn Price

Jones, Frank Campbell	Tŷ Newydd	Pilot S.A.A.F. 34th Squadron

The Memorial Plaque can be seen on the wall on the right. The inscription which heads the plaque reads:

GWELL MARW YN FACHGEN DEWR NA BYW YN FACHGEN LLWFR
(It is better to die young and brave than live as a coward).

This has caused some concern in the past from the clergy and others who considered the wording inappropriate, but the inscription remains.

This plaque lists forty-nine names and homes of men from Llandegla parish who served in the Great War. Of these, five were killed in action in France. Added to this list are the names of two men who lost their lives in the Second World War. It is interesting that all but two of the dwellings named on the Plaque are still standing and occupied. Tan y Graig was damaged by a land mine and never rebuilt (p.65), Tan y Greigiau lies forsaken between Plas Tyno and Rhos Cottage, away from the roadside.

Tan y Greigiau - a forlorn cottage in idyllic countryside
(Janet Handley)

Not all of the names of men from Llandegla who lost their lives in the Great War are listed on this plaque. The diary of Elizabeth Ellis of Tŷ Uchaf records that four of the men whose names appear on the Memorial Plaque were all killed in France:

William Hughes Davies, Mill Cottage (but his home is given as Bryndwr on the Plaque), son of William and Susanah Davies, was killed on the 2nd March 1916;

John Bloor was killed on 3rd July 1916 and his parents were informed on 17th July 1916;

John Parry, the son of Robert and Sarah Parry of Old Gate, was killed on 21st August 1918 and his parents were told on 21st September;

Evan Edwards of the Travellers' Rest Inn (given as the Hand Inn on the Plaque) was killed on 7th October 1918, shortly after *"he was on home leave and his social was on Thursday night, 28th September 1918"*.

The diary also records, in addition to those named above, that John Edwards Hughes of Gloppa was killed in France, the news arriving in Llandegla on 10th May 1917, and also John Jones, son of Tomen yr Adwy, the news of his death arriving on 27th April 1918. The former name is on the Llanfair D.C. memorial, the latter on Bryneglwys. At that time the parish boundaries had just been greatly extended, so there may well have been confusion about which farms were or were not within the new parish boundary.

In addition the Rector's son, Lieut. Ellis, was killed in France. A memorial service was held on 15th May 1917. His home is given as Ysceifiog, which is between Mold and Denbigh.

It took from 1945 to the early 1980's for the Community

The beautiful window erected as a memorial to Glyn Price Jones and Frank Campbell Jones in the Church that they attended. It depicts St George and St Michael 'the patron saints who fight to conquer evil'. *(Janet Handley)*

Council to update the Plaque by adding the two names of those who lost their lives in the Second World War, Frank Campbell Jones and Glyn Price Jones. In May 1947 the Parochial Church Council decided that a memorial in the form of a stained glass window should be erected in the Church in memory of Glyn Price Jones and Frank Campbell Jones. On 14th October 1948 there was a service for the dedication of the window.

The Cenotaph

Unfortunately as the relevant record book has become lost, only a few details of the circumstances surrounding the construction of the Cenotaph are available. Even the person who designed and built it is at present unknown. The 'public subscription' method was probably used to pay for the Cenotaph in the same way as in other local towns and villages.

Between 1920 and March 1922, Llanrheadr, Denbigh County School, Ruthin, Llanrhydd, Denbigh Church, Conwy War Memorial (an obelisk of Welsh granite in the Castle Square), Abergele (at a cost of £600 with seventy-five

The Cenotaph as it is today. The upper plaque commemorates John Bloor, Alexander Cammock, William Hughes Davies, Evan Edwards and John Parry. The lower plaque commemorates Glyn Price Jones and Frank Campbell Jones
(Mrs Jean Wilkinson)

names, standing in the churchyard), Henllan War Memorial, Waen War Memorial and Llansannan were all unveiled, each with a well organised dedication service. Llandegla chose Armistice Sunday in November 1922 to unveil the Cenotaph, which was reported in the Denbighshire Free Press, 16th Nov. 1922, as follows:

"The Unveiling of Llandegla War Memorial

The Memorial for the fallen soldiers from the parish was unveiled at Llandegla last Sunday afternoon. The Memorial, consisting of a broad base of stone, with a beautiful cross of teak wood, stands on the corner of the churchyard where three roads meet - the most prominent place in the parish.

A bilingual service was held in the Parish Church at 2.30p.m., when the church was crowded, many being unable to gain admittance. The hymns were given out, and the first part of the special service was taken by the Rector Rev. J.W.Thomas M.A.. The two lessons and some of the prayers were read by Rev. R.E.Jones, Tregeriog, and the Rev. T.E.Thomas, Coedpoeth. A thoughtful and helpful address appreciated by all and especially by the relatives of the fallen soldiers was given in the church by the Very Rev. Dean of St Asaph. The hymns "O God our help in ages past", "Mor ddedwydd yw y rhai trwy ffydd" and "For all the saints who from their labours rest" were sung in church, Mrs R.H.Jones presiding at the organ. Seats were reserved for the relations of the soldiers who had made the supreme sacrifice, for the ex-soldiers and for the Boy Scouts.

The following was the order of procession passing out of the church: the Clergy, Boy Scouts, ex-soldiers, relations of the fallen soldiers, the congregation.

In front of the Memorial the Scouts, holding a rope, had formed a circle with the ex-soldiers standing on one side of the Memorial and the relatives on the other. Inside the circle stood the clergy and also Capt G.P.Dewhurst, Bodidris, who unveiled the Memorial revealing the large bronze tablet sunk in the stone and bearing the following inscription;

'To the Glory of God, and in memory of the men of this Parish who gave their lives in the great war 1914-1919'

John Bloor, Alexander Cammock, William Hughes Davies, Evan Edwards, John Parry

'Eu henwau fydd byw byth'

The dedication prayers were read by the Very Rev. Dean of St Asaph. An impressive address in English was given by Capt Dewhurst and in Welsh by Rev T.E.Thomas. The Welsh hymn "O Fryniau Caersalem ceir gweled" was then sung and the benediction pronounced by the Dean.

When all had joined in the National Anthem, a large wreath from Capt Dewhurst was placed on the Memorial, one from the ex-soldiers, another from the Boy Scouts and many others from relatives and friends".

Wartime life in Llandegla 1939-45

It was hoped that the Great War would be "the war to end all wars", but we all know how this hope faded with the Second World War. Though Llandegla was relatively remote from the centres of activity it was affected by the privations induced by the war, as was the rest of the country. Fortunately it avoided the mass destruction that affected many of our large towns and cities. Because of the terrible destruction caused by the bombing, many children were evacuated to the country to see them safely through the war. A large number were billeted in Llandegla with their teachers.

Money was needed for the war effort and special events were held frequently, such as War Weapons week, Warships week and Wings for Victory week.

The supply of many consumables during the war was very restricted: the ration book was as essential as money for a shopping trip . Luxuries that we now take for granted, like sweets, were just not available. Rationing ensured a fair distribution of food, which together with an increased production from farms meant that no-one went hungry. Bread was never rationed even though supplies of flour became critically low at times. Vegetables were available, many people responding to the Government's campaign to 'dig for victory' and growing their own. Meals were generally boring but nutritious, people were in a better physical shape than today when foods rich in fat and sugar are readily available. Even though farmers were living where food was being produced everything had to be accounted for: they were restricted to the ration book in the same way as everyone else.

The following example is taken from one person's ration for a week (approx. metric equivalents in brackets):

Bacon & ham	4 oz (113g)	Tea	2 oz (57g)
Sugar	8 oz (227g)	Cheese	1 oz (28g)
Butter	2 oz (57g)	Jam	2 oz (57g)
Cooking fat	8 oz (227g)	Meat	(by price) 1 shilling

(1 shilling was equivalent to 5p but money was worth more then,
5p would be about £1.50 now)
Clothing was scarce, and also rationed by coupons.
Petrol was rationed to 4 - 8 gallons (18 - 36 litres) per month.

There were further restrictions on the general public to help in the war effort. The blackout was designed to make towns and human activity invisible from the air at night when most bombing raids occurred. All windows had to be completely curtained and car headlights were masked to give just enough light forward to drive. It was forbidden to sound car horns and ring church bells: these were only to be used as a warning of invasion. A further regulation was that everyone had to carry an identity card at all times.

All farms were under orders from the War Agricultural Committees, whose field officers came around to beg for food production to be increased at all costs. Much grassland was ploughed up for cropping with grain and potatoes. Farmers were greatly helped by the Women's Land Army and by a large number of prisoners of war. Many of these were billeted on farms while others came from a prisoners' camp at Ruthin. Italians, Poles and Germans all came to Llandegla.

The Home Guard was an unpaid volunteer force made up of men from seventeen to sixty-five who had not been called up for military service. The Home Guard was set up in 1940, as a backup to frontline soldiers when invasion of the UK seemed to be imminent. Though they were the subject of a long-standing TV comedy, they were in fact a well-trained band, uniformed and armed and subject to military discipline. In Llandegla they trained usually every Sunday. Their insistence on the production of identity cards at every road block was a source of annoyance to local residents.

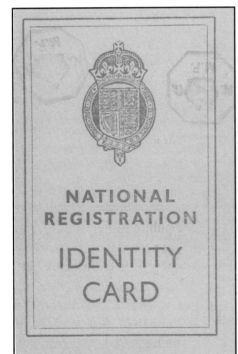

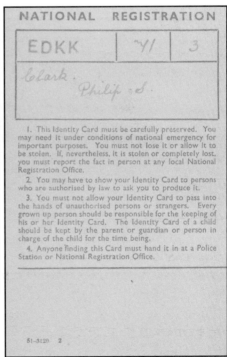

They issued gas masks to everyone under the guidance of air-raid protection personnel.

Cartoons such as this appeared to boost morale.

Jim Turner,
President of
the N.F.U.

423,000
ACRES of POTATOES

Hit him with
this Tom!

We can make it: Heave Tom!

Tom
Williams
Minister of
Agriculture

Herbert
Morrison
?

Clement
Atlee,
Prime
Minister

This well-preserved pill box (a block house officially) stands on the A525 towards Ruthin from the Crown Hotel which can be seen in the background. It is a strong concrete structure with gun ports and internal walls to deflect incoming fire. It would have been built in around 1940 when there was a real threat of invasion, and then manned by the Home Guard. There was usually a member of the home guard on duty by the pill box to guard the bridge.

(Janet Handley)

Mr Vaughan, who lived in the Old Rectory, worked in Liverpool during the war. He was fortunate that he had access to cigarettes: they were like gold in those days. He used to bring fifty home on occasion. His son, unbeknown to him, used to take the opportunity to grab a handful. He and the rest of the gang would then go up to the pill box for an illicit smoke. As the children sat puffing away, the pill box slowly filled with smoke. Eventually there was so much smoke that it started to pour out of the gun ports. This alerted the Home Guard (who was the parent of one of the children) who advanced on the pill box. The children, sensing danger, dived out of the pill box, under the bridge and out the other side, escaping unseen across the fields, leaving the pill box full of smoke but no children. (*As recounted by Mrs Rhianon Lloyd - who was one of the children!*)

Searchlights were one of the weapons used against the German bombers. Their beams of light lit up enemy aircraft making them easily visible to our fighter pilots and anti-aircraft gunners. One of these was located at Perthichwareu and another at Pennant Isaf. Two bombs were targeted at Perthichwareu but exploded near to Chweleiriog Goch. One of these craters was used as a cattle pond (now drained), the other as a rubbish tip. This incident is remembered locally as the Hession children were just being bathed in front of the fire when they were suddenly covered with soot shaken down by the blast. A gap in a hedge is the only remaining evidence of the searchlight at Perthichwareu.

There was a radar station on Cyrn y Brain, the foundations of which can still be seen (p.129). Bombers from the USA sent over to help in the war effort were guided by the radar beam towards the airfield where they were to land. The Germans also used radar. Their bombers followed a radar beam then dropped their bombs where a beam crossed another one. This radar station managed to interfere with the German radar beams so that the German bombers were diverted from their proper targets, the towns and cities.

A special target for the German bombers was Monsanto at Acrefair who were manufacturing chemicals essential for the war effort. To protect the factory a decoy was set up. Lights were erected on the moors around Ruabon Mountain where no-one was living. The remains of a building which housed the generator can still be seen on the moors above Cae Llwyd reservoir near Rhosllanerchrugog. It used to be well-known locally because children playing truant from school went there. When a

RAF Transmitter Station
Horseshoe Pass
Llangollen 1944

The Radar Station on Cyrn y Brain in 1944, taken by George Smith who was on the staff at the time. The foundations for the living quarters and service area and the station itself can be seen (and visited) from the Ponderosa (p.127-129). There are still a few pieces of mast nearby and higher up Cyrn y Brain, which can be recognised by the row of attachments for the fixing of wires. *(Mr John Clemence)*

raid was due the factory lights were shaded as much as possible and the moors lit up. The decoy was effective: the moors were bombed. The bombs set the moors alight, attracting even more bombers which would otherwise have hit targets that mattered. The fires also burned on Moel Garegog on the other side of the A525 but these were lit by the Home Guard. As an additional decoy, temporary buildings were erected on the site of the Clay Pigeon Shooting Club which is an old quarry.

Though the decoy was well outside the parish the fires spread right across to here and four cottages on the fringe of this area suffered bomb damage; Ddôl Ddu, Tan y Graig, Hafod Dafolog and Pen Dinas. At Ddôl Ddu most of the damage was to the outbuildings which were subsequently repaired (p.170). Hafod Dafolog, on the opposite side of the A525 at the beginning of the steep valley running south from the road, suffered blast damage. This cottage has now gone, but not because of the bomb. Tan y Graig was to be the keeper's cottage of the Bodidris Estate. Much of the damage was to the roof which needed to be completely reslated, but also all of the glass was shattered and ceilings

Tan y Graig in happier times, probably in the early 1900s. The field of hay has just been cut with scythes. Pen Dinas is hidden in the trees above Tan y Graig. Mr Robert Jones and Mrs Sarah Jones are in the foreground. *(Mr Bob Robson)*

damaged. The War Damage Commission estimated that repairs would cost £82/6/0 (around £2400 in today's money). The Bodidris Estate had intended to raise the roof to give more headroom upstairs. As the estate had no need for a gamekeeper during the war it was decided to carry out reinstatement or improvement after the war was over. In the event this was never done and Tan y Graig is now a ruin on the opposite side of the A 525 to Tyn y Mynydd.

It was Pen Dinas that seems to have suffered most extensive damage, costing £115 (£3450 today). Doug Garside, nine years old, was asleep in Pen Dinas when the bomb exploded. He remembers what happened:

"It was blackberry time, I would guess October 1941. By a lucky stroke my father had put up the heavy window cover that my brother-in-law had made from galvanised sheets on a wooden frame. My parents and Janet, my elder sister, were having a cocoa and blackberry pie before going to bed when the landmine exploded. Every window in the house was blown in but the cover

took most of the shock in the kitchen and no-one was really hurt. The roof of the house lifted and came back down.

The week before my niece had been staying with us, I had been turfed out of my bed to make room for her. As she was aged about two, my mother put an armchair to stop her rolling out of bed. She went home a couple of days beforehand and I returned to my bed. The chair was still in place. I was a deep sleeper and as a nine-year-old had been in bed for an hour or so. My mother shouted but got no reply. When she got upstairs I was still fast asleep. I had one splinter of glass in my forehead, the armchair and the wooden panelling behind the bed were covered with glass splinters.

To go back before the land mine, if there was a bad raid we used to do down the field to Pete Robson, the shepherd, who lived in Tan y Graig, as they had a cellar (my father by the way was a grouse keeper). After the explosion we started down the field. As we got halfway down we were walking on soil. Pete Robson was coming up from the main road, having taken his son Victor to his brother Matt Robson at Tynymynydd. My father shouted to Pete, "Where did the bomb drop, Pete?" to which came the reply, "Somewhere where the house used to be". Part of the parachute was in the top of a tree and there is still a large piece of the landmine embedded in an ash tree. If my memory serves me right, we spent the night with Idris and Mary Edwards, Casgan Ditw. A few days later my father found a parachute by Pen Dinas Pool. It was brought to Pen Dinas and reported to the authorities. Captain Milne Harrop and I think the police inspector from Ruthin took it away. It had broken away from the partner land-mine which buried itself in the Mill field. This one was later det-onated by a bomb disposal team. As far as I am aware landmines were carried one under each wing, and had to be dropped at the same time".

This particular night was at the end of October 1941. The weather had cleared, allowing the Luftwaffe bombers a free range over North Wales and North and East England. The damage inflicted could have been much worse. A landmine (the other one of the pair) landed, but failed to explode, in a field behind the village school near to St Tecla's Well and an unexploded bomb was found at Chweleiriog Goch. The latter was probably part of the attempt to put out the searchlight at Perthichwareu. Both were defused. The landmine was exhibited in the village on a lorry - the relieved and grateful villagers plied the bomb disposal squad with "lashings of tea"!

Apart from the foundations of the radar station (pp.64, 129) there are two other war relics in Llandegla. Just past the Plough on the A525 towards Wrexham there is an unloading ramp. This was built to unload military vehicles from lorries. Two gun ports can be seen in the wall of the beer garden in the Crown Hotel. These overlook the A5104 towards Corwen and Llangollen and the fields below Raven Farm (investigating Llandegla's war relics is a good excuse for a pint!).

One soldier's story

The following has been written by Kathleen ('Peggy') White about her brother Frank Campbell Jones. It might seem invidious to single out just one of all those who died, but it is in recognition that each would have had their own story and aspirations that were cut short by the war.

"Frank was born in Wantage on August 6th 1922 and spent the first three weeks of his life there, the rest of his early childhood was spent in the parish of Minera. The family moved to the Crown Hotel, Llandegla, in July 1932 where his parents were the proprietors for three years. By this time he had two little sisters, Kathleen Rosemary known as Peggy and Hilda Elizabeth known as Betty. At that time a cattle market was held in the field opposite the Crown. Petrol was sold there and Frank soon took on the job of serving the motorists by manually pumping the pumps.

One day he was sitting on a stile near the rectory playing tunes on his mouth organ when a young man came along and started chatting to him. He then gave Frank his mouth organ (which was far superior to Frank's). The young man turned out to be a student who was staying at the rectory and being taught Greek by the Rector, the Reverend John William Thomas. He was Haile Selassie's nephew from Ethiopia.

In 1935 the family moved to Tegla Cottage. The Church and the village school had an excellent choir. Frank was often chosen to sing solos at concerts and festivals, he also sang a solo at a festival held at St Asaph's cathedral. When the National Eisteddfod was being prepared at Denbigh for the summer of 1939, he was chosen out of all the participating grammar schools to sing a solo there, but before that even took place, he had taken the entrance exam and was awarded a scholarship to the R.A.F. College at Cranwell.

In March 1939 the family moved to Tŷ Newydd. War broke out. Frank trained as an instrument repairer and was stationed at Market Drayton aerodrome. He was able to get home more often and often cycled there and back.

In the early summer of 1941 he left England for an unknown destination. He had his nineteenth birthday on board ship, and finally landed in Capetown, South Africa. Most of his time there was spent in training air force men in the maintenance of aeroplanes. The South African people were most hospitable to the boys and invited them to their homes for weekends etc. One family in particular 'adopted' him and the younger daughter Noelle corresponded with Frank's mother for more than fifty years. Every Christmas for more than forty years she sent flowers to Frank's mother who always placed some in the Memorial Window. Noelle visited Llandegla church in 1978.

Frank was getting homesick by 1943 and felt that he should be doing more to help the war effort. He knew a lot of South African Air Force men were being sent to Europe, so he transferred to the SAAF 34th Squadron. He was sent to the Middle East instead of

Britain much to his disappointment. Six weeks later he was posted to Italy where he began flying on night raids. It was during his fifth flight in the Liberator, on the night of 21st October 1944, that he and the crew in the Liberator were reported missing, presumed killed, over Hungary. It was not until 1947 that his family learned that his crashed plane had been located near Srzombathely and that he and the rest of the crew had been buried in a mass grave at Budapest Military Cemetery. They later learned that each member had been allocated a grave, and a stone memorial erected to each one. The graves are well maintained and in a lovely setting surrounded by hills."

Above: Frank Campbell Jones
aged 18 months
(Mrs Kathleen White)

BUCKINGHAM PALACE

The Queen and I offer you our heartfelt sympathy in your great sorrow.

, We pray that your country's gratitude for a life so nobly given in its service may bring you some measure of consolation.

George R.I.

Mrs. H. F. Jones.

Above: The note of condolence from His Majesty King George VI   *(Mrs Kathleen White)*

Left: Frank Campbell Jones aged 21
(Mrs Kathleen White)

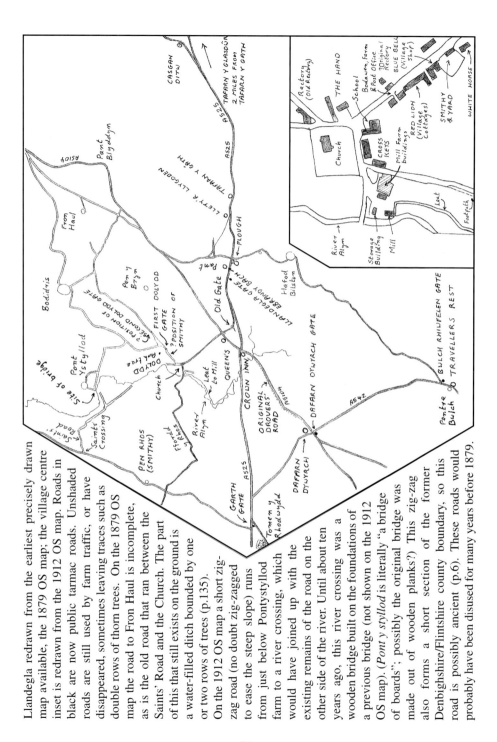

Llandegla redrawn from the earliest precisely drawn map available, the 1879 OS map; the village centre inset is redrawn from the 1912 OS map. Roads in black are now public tarmac roads. Unshaded roads are still used by farm traffic, or have disappeared, sometimes leaving traces such as double rows of thorn trees. On the 1879 OS map the road to Fron Haul is incomplete, as is the old road that ran between the Saints' Road and the Church. The part of this that still exists on the ground is a water-filled ditch bounded by one or two rows of trees (p.135).

On the 1912 OS map a short zig-zag road (no doubt zig-zagged to ease the steep slope) runs from just below Pontystyllod farm to a river crossing, which would have joined up with the existing remains of the road on the other side of the river. Until about ten years ago, this river crossing was a wooden bridge built on the foundations of a previous bridge (not shown on the 1912 OS map). (*Pont y styllod* is literally "a bridge of boards"; possibly the original bridge was made out of wooden planks?) This zig-zag also forms a short section of the former Denbighshire/Flintshire county boundary, so this road is possibly ancient (p.6). These roads would probably have been disused for many years before 1879.

71

5. PAST AND PRESENT: THE VILLAGE

A surprising amount of 'old Llandegla' is still standing, but newer buildings in different styles have given the village a more cosmopolitan atmosphere. Just as the old turf construction gave way to stone, stone has given way to newer materials such as brick and breeze block. These developments have increased comfort for the inhabitants as well as providing dwellings at an affordable cost.

Traditional Welsh cottages were whitewashed, usually annually. The Village Cottages are an example. This custom has been reflected recently in the modern houses of Plas Teg and Ffynnon Tegla but not in most new developments. One can argue that subsequent styles of house building have reduced the visual character of the village, but one can also appreciate that each development reflects its own era. Sometimes colour was added to the whitewash, thus Tŷ Coch (Red House) was probably at one time painted with red coloured whitewash.

It is easy to look back to 'the good old days' and imagine that it would have been idyllic living in a white-painted thatched cottage in the country. This dream is a long way from real life as it would have been then: it was hard for the cottagers with long hours and little pay. Not only that but the services that we now take for granted were generally not available. The good part of the 'old days' was a rich social life.

Old Llandegla village

Church Terrace was built around 1866, about the same time that the Church was being reconstructed. It was once called Time Street Cottages because of the clock on the adjacent school (p.162): it is listed as such in the 1881 census. Both the 'new' school and Church Terrace were built in a field known as *Erw Ysgubor* (Barn Acre). No.1 (nearest to the camera) was the first Police House, which moved up the village hill in 1938. The letter box now in the front door of No.2 was originally in the door of No.1: all police houses had to have a letter box. This one is made of cast

(Janet Handley)

iron, and was the first letter box in Llandegla.

(Phil Clark)

There have been three rectories in Llandegla. The second of these, now called the **Old Rectory**, was built in 1760. According to a recently discovered plaque, the reconstruction of part of this building took place in 1853. It became a rectory in 1880, replacing the original rectory which was on the site of Maes Teg (p.78) opposite the village shop. The house, outbuildings and one acre of land, together with garden and glebe (church land) was granted by Sir William Grenville Williams, Baronet, of Bodidris "as a Parsonage" (actually a rectory). The rector occupied the main house, the small cottage at the other end was let to the Misses Shaw.

The main house appears to have been added to an adjacent earlier long house. (The Leyland Arms at Llanelidan was similarly enlarged, as was possibly Hafod Bilston.) The small cottage at the far end was probably for a farm worker (it was still a working farm while it was a rectory). The bedroom of this cottage was over the central section of the old building, once a cattle byre and latterly used as a coach house (as noted in the deeds of 1940). At some time this cottage was extended at the back, adding a kitchen and bathroom. When this extension was demolished recently the remains of a pig sty were found. It was usual for pigs to be kept near to the house for food and income and the sty would have been a convenient structure to build on to.

To coincide with the extension of the parish boundaries (pp.4-8), a new, grander Rectory was built between 1925 and 1927, less conveniently, on the other side of the river from the Church. It resembles Plas Tyno, further down the road, which was built at the same time and designed by the same architect. (Plas Tyno was built on a greenfield site for the Bodidris estates manager, Mr Rathbone. When the estate was sold up, the then agent, Mr Moon, bought the house in which he was living.)

The last rector to live in the Old Rectory was the Reverend J W Thomas who was Rector from 1916 until 1941. There is a plaque to his memory in the Children's Corner in the Church. He married late, which may account for the date of the sale of the Old Rectory. It was sold in 1925 by the Church in Wales to Mr E Johnson, a retired stationmaster from Leicester, as a private dwelling house. Mr Johnson sold the small cottage

An aerial view of the church (left), the Old Rectory (centre) and the Hand (right) taken in 1971. The lane past the Church, Ffordd Fain, goes to the old sewage works at the top of the picture, the Offa's Dyke Path carries straight on past the sewage works. The lane on the right gives access to Pontystyllod Farm in about a mile. The Hand is bottom right with the sycamore tree in front. The long farm building behind the Hand, an old shippon, has recently been converted into cottages called Trem yr Eglwys. The corrugated iron shed has now gone.
(Reproduced with permission from Mr. R P Jones, Dragon Aviation, Wrexham.)

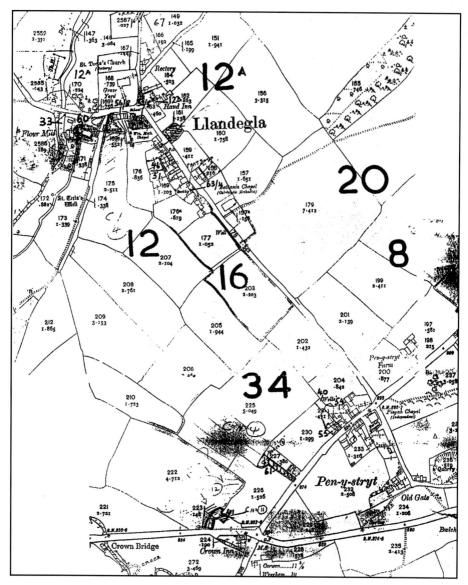

Llandegla and Pen y Stryt photocopied from the 1912 OS map (reduced). Scale: approximately 500 yards between The Square (between the School and The Hand) and the crossroads at Pen y Stryt. (This map was one of a number used to identify fields and properties when the Dewhurst family sold the Bodidris estate in 1958 (p.154), hence the additional marks on this copy.) In the ninety years between this map and the one opposite, the major losses have been the farm buildings opposite Bodawen and those associated with the Hand.

75

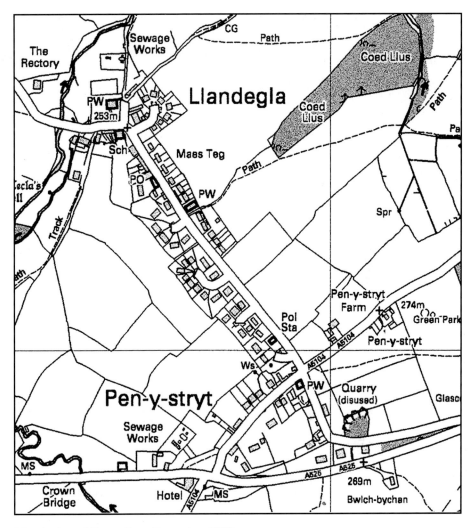

Llandegla and Pen y Stryt December 2000.
Note how the new estates (the 'infill') are contained within the old field boundaries.
The police station has now closed.
+ = the height above sea level in metres
PW - place of worship (the church and the two chapels)
MS - milestone
Ws - wells (now filled in, these were the water supply for Pen y Stryt)

to Ethel Vaughn in 1940. The cottage was then known as Rectory Cottage, but is now known as *Diddosfa* (Sheltered Place). The occupiers in 1962 changed the name of the Old Rectory to *Gorphwysfa* (sic) (Resting Place), but the subsequent owners changed it back to the Old Rectory in 1979. Its most recent owners, the Wylies, have also acquired the small cottage and re-integrated it into the rest of the building. A very recent extension has been removed and the coach house is now a kitchen. *(Information from David and Juliette Wylie)*

Another supernatural event well established in Llandegla folk lore concerns the Old Rectory. A poltergeist was making a misery of the life of the occupants of the Old Rectory, by throwing kitchen utensils about, stones around the grounds and clods of earth at passers-by, and by appearing in a different form each night. The Reverend Griffiths from Graianrhyd was asked to exorcise this ghost. He drew two chalk lines on the floor. Standing on one, he commanded the ghost to appear on the other. It did so and took on many horrible forms until Reverend Griffiths succeeded in changing it into a bluebottle which he caught in a small box. He placed this box under a stone under the bridge over the River Alyn. The ghost complained bitterly at being treated like this, so the Reverend relented and told the ghost that when a nearby tree grew as high as the parapet of the bridge he would be free. However the villagers lopped the branches to keep it below the parapet and the ghost confined. This custom was abandoned in the nineteenth century. Though the tree has now grown much taller than the bridge the ghost may still be lingering there as it has not been seen since.

As already mentioned, the Memorial Hall was originally a Wesleyan Chapel, opened in 1842. The two white houses to the left of the Hall were, until the late 1980's, one large house known as **Bodawen**. This was formerly a farm, with the farm buildings (now demolished) on the opposite side of the road which eventually housed the generator for Llandegla's electricity supply. It was also Llandegla's Post Office until it moved to the Bluebell and then to the Pioneer Stores on Pen y Stryt just after the First World War (p.83). Bodawen had been bought by the Hall Committee. The caretaker of the Hall used to live there. However in the

'80s both Bodawen and the Hall were in need of need of extensive repairs. After a long and hard discussion it was agreed to sell Bodawen to Tai Clwyd Housing Association who renovated it and made it into two houses. Opportunity was also taken to widen the narrow access to the Hall Field between Bodawen and the Hall by moving back the entire gable end of Bodawen.

Bodawen before renovation around 1990 *(Janet Handley)*

The Village Cottages date from the late 1600's; the remains of a post and panel dividing wall (vertical slotted posts with wooden panels fitted in between) have been found which is characteristic of the period. These Cottages appear to replace older buildings which may well have had turf walls (as Dafarn Dywyrch, p.99) and been roofed with thatch. There

The Village Cottages. The houses on the right are Maes Teg, built early post-war. The original rectory (before the Old Rectory) used to be on this site. Beyond is the gable end of the Hand. *(Janet Handley)*

The village street (*Stryt yr Efail* or Smithy Street) around 1900. There are no post office signs, so the Bluebell Inn has probably not yet become the Post Office. On the left is part of the Old Smithy. The building behind the cart was probably a wash-house. Behind this, out of sight, was a pair of cottages which may originally have been one dwelling, the original rectory before the rector moved to the Old Rectory in 1880. These buildings have now gone, Maes Teg occupies the site. *(Memorial Hall)*

The same view around 1920. The gable end of The Hand can be distinguished with its chimney (the fire in the bar used to draw beautifully!). The farm buildings in the

background on the right belonged to Bodawen (just out of our view, behind the Village Cottages). These have now gone. They housed the generator that replaced the turbine (pp.113-115).

(Mrs and Mrs K.Bellis)

79

may have been as many as eight cottages in the complex, but due to mergers, there are now only three. Behind the Cottages there was a communal green (now a private garden) with access from the road, probably where No.5 is now, as this cottage appears to be an infill. At the back there is (still!) a brick bread oven and a communal wash house with a copper. The small cottage (No.8) is known as Accre View (Moel yr Accre can be seen from a window). It

Mrs 'Nain' Roberts

was owned by Accre Hall, unlike the rest which were owned by the Bodidris Estate. Mrs Elizabeth Roberts, known to everybody as 'Nain', lived at No. 3 much of her married life. She baked bread in the brick oven and sold it to the villagers for a penny a loaf. She died in 1972 aged eighty nine.

The Old Smithy *(Janet Handley)*

Immediately above the Village Shop is the Old Smithy, the only one of the original drovers' smithy buildings left in Llandegla. It is now a garage and workshop.

Old Pen y Stryt

Pen y Stryt was a village separate from Llandegla, there were open fields between. It had its own shops, pub and chapel. Coffins were made and coal was sold in the sheds behind London House, cattle feed was sold in bags from Belle View, there was a butcher's shop in what is now Rose Cottage and a doctor's surgery in Rose Moor Cottage.

Overleaf is an early photograph of Pen y Stryt, looking up from

Llandegla. Pisgah Chapel faces the camera, with London House on the right. The building on the right belongs to Rose Cottage, being used at

various times as a store room, bath room and so on. It then became a garage and was eventually demolished. Old Gate Lane runs past the left of Pisgah Chapel, the present A5104 passes between Pisgah Chapel and London House.

(Above, Mr Owen)   *(Below, Phil Clark)*

The second view is taken from the same location. More recent developments have obscured the previous view. The building partly hidden by the Leylandii conifers is now a private

A group of friends in Old Gate Lane, probably in the late 1930s. Brynhyfryd's gate is on the left, the gable end behind the cattle shed (now demolished) is Tan y Bryn. Left to right: Hugh Lloyd; Mr Pritchard, Tan y Bryn; Joseph Goodman; a visitor, Joseph Williams; Daniel Roberts, Yr Hen Giât. The dog on the bicycle at the back is Bob, who belonged to Meredydd Evans, the postman. *(Mrs Flora Edwards)*

residence, but was a police house until 1993: the home of the village bobby. This was built in 1938. (Previously this was No.1 Church Terrace). The house beyond this is Llys Myfyr (Court of Studying) which housed ministers for Bethania chapel.

Below is an early view of Pen y Stryt looking uphill. London House (1890) is on the left, Rose Cottage adjacent hidden by bushes. It used to

be a butcher's shop. Pen y Stryt Cottages are on the right, beyond Pisgah Chapel hidden by bushes. The crossroads is at the end of the wall past London House.

(Mrs Sandra Williams-Blythen)

(Janet Handley)

Above is the same view today. Little has changed, except that London House appears to have been extended: there is an extra window. This extension is actually on a separate dwelling, Rose Cottage. Pisgah Chapel can be seen beyond Pen y Stryt Cottages. In the distance on the right is a barn belonging to Green Park, on the left is Pen y Stryt Farm.

(Janet Handley)

Another modern view looking up Pen y Stryt from farther downhill towards the Crown. London House can be seen in the distance. Before this are Queens Cottages, built on the site of the Queens Inn for the workers on the Bodidris Estate (p.99). Belle View is behind the wall behind the cherry tree (front left). Animal feed used to be sold from here before the establishment of the Pioneer Stores, now the Willows (behind the camera on the right).

The Pioneer Stores

Following the Great War of 1914-18, Mr T P Smith, an exserviceman, built what was later to become the Pioneer Stores and Post Office on a

piece of roadside waste land (the Post Office moved here from the old Bluebell (p.90). Mr Smith also generated electricity for the Pen y Stryt area (p.113) and wired houses for electricity.

Mr and Mrs T P Smith
(Mr W Owen)

Mr T P Smith's postcard (c1920) of the Pioneer Stores. This view is looking down the A5104 towards the Crown Hotel *(Mrs Rhianon Lloyd)*

Mrs Sylvia Jones (nee Sylvia Beech) outside the Pioneer Stores when she worked there 1937-38 *(Mrs Sylvia Jones)*

Extended, and in its final state as a post office *(Mrs Flora Edwards)*

After Mr T P Smith retired a young couple, Mr and Mrs Jones, took over the shop. They were followed by Mr and Mrs Browness. Mrs Browness ran a nursery school there on two afternoons a week. Mr and Mrs Barnbrook then ran the shop. They had five children. Mrs Barnbrook converted the store room into a hairdressing salon, and also started making teas. They moved to Grimsby after naming the tea shop The Copper Kettle.

Finally, about twenty five years ago, Mr and Mrs Phil Owen acquired The Copper Kettle and enlarged the catering business into The Willows as it is today. The post office and shop moved back down into what used to be the Blue Bell Inn (pp.83, 90).

The Willows today, looking up from the Crown Hotel. The section nearest to the camera was the original Pioneer Stores *(Mrs Janet Robinson)*

The Crown Sawmill   *(Jane and David Alcock)*

Evidence from maps suggests that the Crown Sawmill was built shortly before 1850. Tithe maps show no sign of the property but it appears on the proposed Ruthin railway link map of 1850. Another clue is the presence of the toll stone (p.37) found at the threshold of a downstairs room, as the tollgates were being taken down around that time and stone re-used. (It is interesting to speculate where this came from. Both of the local tollhouses are still shown on the 1879 map, and according to the 1871 census the Bwlch Rhiwfelen Gate was still occupied by a family of seven. Another possibility is a toll house on the old road to Ruthin via Graigfechan: any tollgate on that road would have suffered a dramatic loss of income once the road through Nant y Garth had been constructed.) The original name was probably Buarth Ucha (Upper Farmyard), being built on a farm (the present name comes from its location opposite the Crown Hotel). It may have been built by the Bodidris Estate as a wheelwright's shop: the estate subsequently established their timber yard and had their carpentry shop here, moving their mobile steam sawmill operation from the surrounding forest and woods. In the 1940's the ground floor was owned by the Rennies from the Plough (p.98) and then by the Moss family as part of the Wrexham sawmill operation. On the upper floor joinery continued to be done for the estate.

It was purchased by Jane and David Alcock in December 1994 in a

run down and derelict state. The stone building was the original building, built in yellowy orange sandstone with lime mortar joints and lime and horsehair plaster. Various

(Flora Edwards)

86

modifications had altered its appearance but the basic structure was very sound, with a high standard of craftsmanship in the stonework internally and externally. Historically, it was split into four main sections: accommodation, stabling, forge room with two forges on the ground floor, and carpentry shop on the first floor with two other smaller rooms possibly for a wood storage/drying area and a bellows or engine room. All were under the one roofline, with no indication of parts being added to the original building at later dates.

The forge room appears to have been the most significant room in the original plan. This room contained two chimney flues positioned four feet off the ground, one backing on to the dwelling chimneybreast and the other in an internal wall. These raised flues probably accommodated two free-standing forges, built of brick or cast iron, with hoods to direct the fumes up the flue. A small hole nine by nine inches in the back wall may indicate that the room at the back of the property contained bellows or belt and shaft-driven machinery to power the forge. It is unusual to find two forges together, and in a two-storey building. This suggests the building had been constructed for a specific purpose, probably as an industrial unit housing a production line process of some sort, with accommodation for the owner, manager or headworker.

The forges could have manufactured horseshoes, nails, nuts and bolts, gate fittings, door and window fittings, wheel hoops and wagon iron-work. The carpentry shop could have produced doors, windows, gates, wheel parts, and wagon frames. Two artifacts were found, a traditional blacksmith's peg-leg vice (serial number CMS 10634) and a special puller device possibly something to do with cart wheels. Wheelwrights combined the two skills, producing wooden wheels bound with steel hoops all put together on site. A John Elias, wheelwright, resided in the village in 1864: perhaps he owned the property or worked here?

Stone steps at the south end, which had a dog kennel built into them, led to a large open room with low roof trusses above the forge and stables. This was the carpentry shop in years past and still retained the bench and vice (which are being utilized now for the rebuild operations). It must have been the warmest place in Llandegla in winter with the forges going, but a hot house in summer. The steps pass a door at the bottom which may have been a storage/drying room for wood: vents from the room upstairs lead into it, high in the roof space.

A double door opening at the front right of the building accessed the stabling area. A stump hole with a lump of wood still remaining was found while digging out slate cobbles. Also oat husks and accurately chopped chaff were found in a hole in the back wall indicating a possible partition. The partitioned area was not of the normal cattle byre layout, but wider, suggesting horse stabling. The horses may have been used for delivery of finished items.

The accommodation, at the northern end of the building, consisted of a living room and one bedroom. The living room was raised some twelve inches above the rest of the property, a common practice in combined domestic and agricultural buildings of the time. Footings were found outside, possibly indicating a wash-house/toilet built up against the house. Timbers in the living room were original and had the bottom corners shaved off, indicating a domestic room. A fitted range incorporated a fire grate, oven and boiler, with what was probably an ash pit in the floor a foot out from the grate, properly built in stone and measuring approximately two foot deep and two foot wide. Lime plaster had been applied between joists under upstairs floorboards and to walls. Whilst renewing the timber lintels above the door and window, it was noticed that the old timbers were parts of a four-wheel wagon, two pieces making up the front turntable, the third piece being the tail end of the wagonbed.

The doorway at the back of this room led to what was probably a scullery with a slate floor and small window to the rear. From here narrow winding stairs led to the only bedroom. Above the scullery was a loft space, which may have been for the children to sleep in! The bedroom had its own fire-grate. The ceiling went up into the rafters of the house. One of the original purlins remains: a tree trunk with roughly sawn down sides but bark remaining at the corners, decorated with a lime-based whitewash, as were the lime-plastered bedroom walls.

David writes:

"Having owned the sawmill for five years, site developments are slowly coming to fruition. We won the best Llandegla village garden for the year 2000! The stone building is being converted into domestic accommodation, whilst the old steel building is being renovated for use as a four-wheel drive workshop, establishing Packhorse 4x4 (a modern version of the local black-smith/wheelwright) as the latest business on the site. We are retaining as many features as possible, re-establishing old designs and incorporating new ones as sympathetically as possible, using only stone and a lime based mortar in wall renovations. Rotten timbers have been replaced with sound timbers rather than steel lintels (some of the large replacement timbers in the new living room came secondhand from the Liverpool garden exhibition site). We reopened the stable archway which had been roughly filled in, with the key stone going in at midnight on the 31st December 1999/2000 while the chimes of Big Ben rang in the New Millennium. We are now becoming part of its history".

The drovers' pubs

Of the sixteen pubs which used to serve the drovers, only two still remain as pubs: the Plough and the Crown Hotel. There were five in the village itself: the Cross Keys, the White Horse, the Blue Bell, the Red Lion and the Hand.

The Cross Keys: The Cross Keys and Mill Farm were a pair of cottages. By 1881 the Cross Keys had closed as a pub. It was a farm of just five acres, Mill Farm being twenty-seven acres. Later the pair of cottages was made into one dwelling - the present Mill Farm.

The White Horse is now White Horse Cottage, behind which is the modern housing development of Plas Teg.

The White Horse in about 1868
(Mrs Rhianon Lloyd)

In 1999, as a private cottage
(Janet Handley)

The Blue Bell was still a pub in 1891. Three pine trees denoted its location. It is now the village shop and post office. It is not known when the Post Office moved to the Bluebell from Bodawen, but below we see the horse mail arriving at the Post Office in about 1900.

(Mrs and Mrs K.Bellis)

The Red Lion is now part of the Village Cottages. Which of the cottages was the inn is uncertain, but it was possibly No 4 as there is a hatchway in the wall facing the street (not visible from the outside) which could have been used as a serving hatch.

The Hand only closed as a pub after a fire in 1986. It is now a private house but the present building dates from the rebuilding of 1739.

The Hand, 1925 (Denbighshire Record Office)

The Hand basking in the winter sunshine in February 2001 behind the skeletal form of its sycamore tree. The conversion of the old shippon into cottages is now complete. Further to the right the church wall, Cenotaph and roof of the Old Rectory are in view *(Phil Clark)*

An original painting of the Hand in 1973 by Herbert Parker. (*reproduced with permission from Gill Kingston*)

Calling Card: Above, the front showing the main bar of the Hand as it was in about 1980, ready to welcome its customers. Below, the inside giving details of local events held at the Hand   *(Mrs Rhianon Lloyd)*

This is a fine Fifteenth Century Inn situated 18 miles from Chester and 10 miles from Wrexham.	FREE HOUSE.
FUNCTIONS & PARTIES CATERED FOR	**The Hand Inn**
Meals provided — Supper License	**Llandegla**
Musical evening every night except Monday and Tuesday.	**Nr. Wrexham**
	Denbighshire
Come and join us in our homely atmosphere. JEAN & BILL.	Telephone - - Llandegla 206

On the Wrexham Road (A525) were six more pubs: Llety'r Llygoden, Tafarn y Gâth, Casgan Ditw, Tafarn y Glasdŵr, Ebrandy Bach and the Plough.

Llety'r Llygoden has been rebuilt as a private house. The name means 'the mouse's lodgings'.

Tafarn y Gâth means 'the cat's tavern'. Early maps use this name but later OS maps (1986, 1991) label it as Tafarn y Garth. Garth means an enclosure in Welsh as it does in English. It seems that a recent mistake in the name has unfortunately persisted, so losing a little bit of history. There used to be a cat painted on the wall facing Casgan Ditw. It is now a farm and butcher's shop selling home-grown meat.

(Both photographs taken by Janet Handley: permission to reproduce photograph of Tafarn y Gath from Dorothy Pluke)

Casgan Ditw means 'hated by the bird (a tit)'. The bird hates the cat; the two inns were in competition with each other. Casgan Ditw is now a private house and

fish farm. During recent renovations, corn and pieces of hay were found behind the plaster upstairs. The gable end facing the road originally had a wide opening as if carts used to be stored in the present lounge. There were six chimneys but only five fireplaces in the house, the sixth chimney was for the fire that heated the tar for tarring the feet of geese to protect them as they went on the drove (this was also done at the Raven and the Traveller's Rest).

A small stream runs along the hedgerow (upper right of the photograph): the headwaters of Yr Alun Bach. This was the old parish boundary (p.7). Casgan Ditw itself was in the parish of Llandegla but the field to the top

An aerial view of Casgan Ditw in 1971 when it was still a farm, before the trout ponds were excavated in the late seventies. The barn and other outbuildings have since been demolished and a new entrance made further down the road which is the A525.
(Reproduced with permission from Mr R.P. Jones, Dragon Aviation, Wrexham)

94

right of the photograph was in Llanarmon parish. There are numerous springs around the farm and on the slope above so there is a very adequate water supply for the trout ponds. A conspicuous feature nowadays is a well in the car park near to the road. It supplies domestic water ("the water is beautiful"). As it is at a constant 9°C it is pumped into the trout ponds at times to warm the water in winter and cool them in summer.

There used to be a loop of road that ran behind Abergroes Farm on the Old Road. **Tafarn y Glasdŵr** was on this road just behind the farm. The road has now gone, being incorporated into the neighbouring fields. *Glasdŵr* means blue water, that is, buttermilk diluted with water. After the milk had been churned to make butter, this was the milk left over. As some of the pubs did not brew their own beer, buttermilk was served instead. It was last known to be occupied in the 1930's. There is little left of the pub. The part that was standing but derelict has been converted into a stable in recent times.

Ebrandy Bach is now Tegla Cottage. *Ebran* refers to a food for horses: oats, bran, chopped straw and water, mixed and stood for 24 hours, then mixed again. This mix avoided colic. *Tŷ (Dŷ) bach* means small house.

On old maps it was shortened to 'Brandy' but it had acquired its present name by 1879. Miss Crook and Miss Gibbs lived there during the early part of the war. They held religious services in the end bedroom, where there were hooks in the ceiling for banners. In the shed in the front garden they had ready a bed, candle and food for the

When Irene and Fred Edwards first lived in Tegla Cottage they ran a small café, so there is an 'open' sign in the window in this photograph taken in 1967. They also provided bed and breakfast for visitors. *(Mrs Irene Edwards)*

'gentlemen of the road'. Mrs Menna Hubbard lived in Tegla Cottage with her family between 1943 and 1948.

Above: Fred Edwards serving a customer at Tegla Garage, 1995. *(Janet Handley)*

1967: Martin Edwards aged three calls in at his father's garage. *(Mrs Irene Edwards)*

The garage has now been rebuilt as a workshop where Fred's son Martin manufactures quality hand made furniture.The petrol pumps have now gone. *(Mrs Janet Robinson)*

The Plough is still in use

(Mr Tegla Jones, Mrs Menna Hubbard)

This postcard, published by T P Smith, Pioneer Stores (p.83) shows the Plough before it was altered and much extended. The door on the left leads to the gents. The building centre right is Yale Garage, in front of this was the first petrol pump in Llandegla. Both the Plough and the garage were owned by the Harrison family. Later the garage moved across the road to Tegla Cottage where it was built up by the Vaughn family. (Petrol was also sold from opposite the Crown Hotel, the foundations for these pumps can still be seen.)

Above is The Plough photographed in 1999. The A525 is to the right, the road on the left goes to Hafod Bilston. *(Janet Handley)*

The Harrisons were succeeded at the Plough by the Rennies. Derek Rennie remembers life thus:

'My father was John James Rennie always known as Jack. He bought the Plough Inn from the Harrison family in the early 40's and a little later bought the Crown Sawmill.

We were a family of five when we moved in and two more children arrived on the scene. We were always nicknamed the five D's - Dennis, Doreen, Derek, Delia and Dianne. There were seventeen years between the eldest Dennis and the youngest Dianne, and as the family had grown my father bought Tegla Cottage which was across the road. That meant we had more living accommodation and more land, increasing the acreage to approximately fifty acres. We were running the Plough as a farm as well and we had two petrol pumps on the forecourt with a garage. It was a very busy life as my father was also running a timber business.

When we first moved in the only lighting we had were tilley lamps. We then progressed to our own generator which also provided electricity in Tegla Cottage. At that time Llandegla village had its own dam, pump house and power station which was situated down past the Hand Pub, and it was maintained by Dan Jones known as "Dan Bach".

There were some very likeable characters in the village who either worked or socialised in our pub (or did both). There was "Dai Old Gate", "Ted Bach", "Griff the Roadman", Stanley Harrison who moved next door, Mr Grace who kept the Hand in the village, who also used to slaughter pigs for us, Mr Griff Price who lived at Tŷ Ucha and had a little shed on his property where we used to take our shoes to be repaired, and I will never forget "John y Botel" who used to arrive at the Plough off the bus at 6 o'clock, have a game of dominoes with either my mother or father, and depart on the 7 o'clock bus complete with a pint bottle of beer, hence the nickname.

The pubs in earlier years always closed at 10 o'clock. My mother would put the towels on the bar to close for the evening and then retire to bed, and my father would then say to his regulars "Open again at ten past ten, lads", which he did. His excuse was that no-one had finished their game of darts or had finished drinking, and he never closed until his customers were ready to go.

On Sunday mornings Ted and Marion Edwards used the Plough car park to sell Sunday newspapers and when they had finished Marion would deliver newspapers on her Corgi autocycle to some customers who could not manage to pick them up. Also, some Sundays it was used by Wrexham Motorcycle Club to run their motorbike trials.

My father died at the Plough in 1957 aged 56 years and my mother died the following year. We then sold the Plough. We all had very happy years in Llandegla, it was and is a lovely village."

There were four pubs on the Chester - Corwen Road (A5104): the Queens Inn, the Raven, Dafarn Dywyrch and the Crown Hotel.

The Queens Inn was rebuilt as two houses for estate workers in 1922 and is now Queens Cottages, Pen y Stryt.

The Raven is now Raven Farm.

Dafarn Dywyrch means 'Turf Tavern' (p.34). Turf used to be a normal material for the construction of cottages as it was readily available and cottagers were unable to afford stone or its transport. Such cottages were often one room only, divided into two by furniture. This pub was visited by George Borrow in 1854. He found it to be "a decent public-house of rather an antiquated appearance". On inquiring about the name, his guide explained "because it was originally a turf hovel. Though at present it consists of good brick and mortar". The ale was so good that he ordered a second jug. It is now a farm.

The Crown Hotel is still in use. It used to be the Crown Inn, and is still shown as such on the 1930 OS map. It is not known when it became the

Crown Hotel. The building itself is listed. During the course of recent renovations the rendering was removed revealing a rather magnificent stone front. It was agreed by all those involved that it would greatly enhance the appearance of the building if the stonework was left uncovered. However, as the Crown Hotel was originally listed as a white building, the rendering had to be replaced, the result giving the impression of white painted breeze blocks.

The Crown Hotel in 1900 *(Denbighshire Record Office)*

The Crown Hotel in 1937 *(Mr Tegla Jones)*

The Crown Hotel in 1999 *(Mrs Janet Robinson)*

In the Crown, late 1960's: Mr Aspen (Irene Edwards' father), Tegla Garage; Alun Davies, Ffynnon Wen; John Hughes, Dafarn Dywyrch and Archie Carr. Archie was one of the village 'characters'. Regret is sometimes expressed that there are no characters now as there used to be, but it seems that the characters of old were moulded by hardship. *(Mr & Mrs K. Bellis.)*

The Crown car park once had a large shed where tractors and other farm machinery were collected together for use during the war. There was a grain drier there as well., manned by Italian prisoners of war. Opposite the Crown was a livestock market, which later moved to the Hand.

Finally, on the Llangollen road (A542) was the **The Traveller's Rest**. This closed as an inn in 1937, and was demolished in 1967. Before Llandegla Parish was enlarged, the parish boundary ran through the inn.

The inn itself was in the Parish of Llandegla, while the stable of the inn was in the Parish of Llantysilio. The site is now a small lay-by, on the left on the way to the Horseshoe Pass, opposite Pentre Bwlch Farm, so it is still a place of rest for travellers.

The Travellers' Rest in the 1930's. A pub, then a café and now gone! *(Mrs Dilys Davies)*

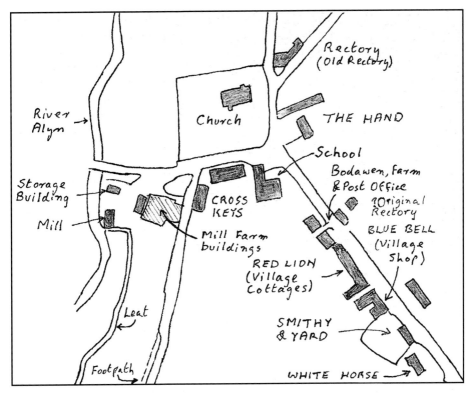

Location of the Drovers' pubs   *(Phil Clark)*

Recent housing developments

Modern developments have filled in the space between the villages of Pen y Stryt and Llandegla, joining them together. From Pen y Stryt to Llandegla village, all the fields adjacent to the road on the left have been used for housing. The names of the estates were chosen by the school children: Pen Lan, Bryn Tegla and Plas Teg. As a separate field was used for each housing estate, the boundaries between the estates are the old field boundaries. The old farm track (Ffordd y Plas) between Bryn Tegla and Plas Teg is still in use.

The Ffynnon Tegla houses, developed by Tai Clwyd in the 1990's, are the latest Llandegla development. Ffynnon Tegla was built on the last remaining field owned by the Hand, which had been an old cattle market.

(All from Janet Handley)

Top: Pen Lan, at the crest of the Village Hill

Upper Middle: Bryn Tegla. The original developers were unable to complete the estate, abandoning it after a house and a bungalow had been built. The estate was subsequently completed between 1984 and 1986. Though pleasing, this variation in houses and bungalows does not reflect vernacular Welsh architecture.

Lower Middle: Plas Teg, built in the late 70's. This estate lies behind the cottage that used to be the White Horse pub. Just on the left of the entrance there used to be a cattle trough, which was destroyed when the estate was started. There are now no cattle troughs in the village: all of these remnants of a former age of transport have disappeared.

Bottom: Ffynnon Tegla.

6. PAST AND PRESENT: THE PARISH

Old Llandegla beyond the village

Roughly half of the population of Llandegla lives in the village itself, the other half is scattered over the rest of the ten square miles that make up our parish. Most of the dwellings are, or were, farms or associated with agriculture in some way. Many of the buildings are old, some very old (for example Plas Newydd - New Place!) with a few new ones added in.

Tai Newyddion (New Houses) cottages were built to house the quarry men who worked in the quarry at the top of the Horseshoe Pass (Moel y Faen). According to David Crane *(Walks through the history of rural Llangollen)*, they were built some time between 1845 and 1875 although one of the buildings could be older and could be the original single dwelling that occupied the site in 1844. Called *Tŷ Twrch* (Mole or Hog House) it was owned and occupied by Edward Edwards. The name indicates that pig farming was one of the means of making a living. This evidently continued after the building of the new houses, as in 1881 William Evans, who then lived there applied for permission to have "2 pig sties and oven at Bwlchrhiwfelen". Tai Newyddion was a community in itself, with a pub (The Travellers' Rest, p.101), a chapel (Salem Pentre Bwlch, p.188) and its own band.

The houses were nearly demolished in about 1980: on learning that the condition of the cottages was so poor, the then Environmental Health Officer of Glyndŵr District Council was giving serious consideration to a Compulsory Purchase Order, which would have meant that the cottages would be demolished and the site cleared. The local member of the District council, Mr William Owen, successfully persuaded the authority to consider bringing in a piped mains water supply from the Bryneglwys road, a distance of approximately three quarters of a mile. It was found to be as cheap to bring in mains water and make other improvements, thus the cottages were saved. The front four cottages are now made into one.

Tai Newyddion before the alterations *(Mrs Dilys Davies)*

After the alterations, photographed in February 1999 *(Janet Handley)*

Though **Pentre Bwlch** dates from around 1600, there was probably a dwelling on the site from much earlier. In the 1700's there was a working mill there where flour was ground. When the present owner started to renovate the house he found a 'wig cupboard', the small cupboard beside the fireplace, and a priest's hole in the chimney of the middle room. (After the introduction of Protestantism in the late sixteenth and seventeenth centuries it was illegal for a Catholic priest to enter the country. If he was found he would be beheaded and the family sheltering him imprisoned. A priest hole was a hiding place into which he could go in times of danger. Bodidris also has one)

Old documents available from the Record Office often turn out to be agreements for the letting of property. Sometimes items of real interest emerge from the flowery and repetitive text. One such document was the letting of Pentre Bwlch Farm to William Ellis of Bwlch in 1787, eighty-six acres for £21 a year, from Sir Edward Lloyd of Pengwern. 'Bwlch' may be Plas y Bwlch, the nextdoor farm, which would have been in the Parish of Llantysilio. Pengwern Hall lies in the valley just southeast of Llangollen. Below is the first part of this agreement:

THIS INDENTURE made the ninth day of march in the year of our Lord one thousand seven hundred and eighty seven and in the twenty seventh year of the Reign of our Sovereign Lord George the third King over Great Britain and so forth. BETWEEN Sir Edward Lloyd of Pengwern in the County of Flint, Baronet, of the one part and William Ellis of Bwlch in the parish of Llantisilio in the County of Denbigh, yeoman of the other part. WITNESSETH that for and in consideration of, the yearly Rents covenants payments and agreements herein after reserved and contained and which on the part and behalf of the said William Ellis, his Executors, administrators and assigns are or ought to be paid kept done and performed and for diverse other good causes and valuable considerations HIM the said Sir Edward Lloyd hereunto especially moving. HE the said Sir Edward Lloyd HATH demised granted set and to farm let unto the said William Ellis, his Executors Administrators and Assigns. ALL that messuage tenement and farm of him the said

Above: the first part of the agreement (demise: grant by lease; messuage: dwelling house with outbuildings attached)

106

In this agreement all of the fields are named. The same names are still in use well over two hundred years later (the Welsh spelling is modern).

Weirglodd Fawr	Big Meadow
Pant yr Onnen	Ash Hollow
Weirglodd Fechan	Small Meadow
Tir Du	Black Land
Rhandir	Allotment
Cae Isa Mawr	Big Lower Field
Cae Isa Bychan	Small Lower Field
Weirglodd y Pentre	Village Meadow
Y Ferm	The Farm
Bryniog Cae Draw	Yonder Hilly Field
Cae Canol	Middle Field
Yr Ardd	The Garden
Cae Pwll y Glo	Coal Mine Field
Pen Isa'r Stryd	The Lower Top of the Street
Erw dan yr Ysgubor	The acre under the barn
Cae o dan y tŷ	Field below the house

There are three fields in the agreement which cannot now be identified: *Waow* (?); *Cae'r Ffynnon* (well field); and *Cae tan y Bedw* (the field below the birch trees).

Not far from Pentre Bwlch is another farm, **Hafod yr Abad**, which probably dates from the fourteenth century. This was reputed to have been the summer residence of the monks from Valle Crucis Abbey. (*Hafod*, often found in Welsh place names, was formerly a summer shelter or cottage used by a family during the summer while sheep were on upland pastures.) It has a long history yet to be properly investigated, a reason for making efforts to keep similar but less fortunate buildings where the history is even less known.

The lay-shaft at Trefydd Bychain is the kind of equipment which would have been found on many farms in former times. The shaft transferred power to run items of farm machinery, such as a turnip slicer (like the one opposite) and chaff cutter (turnips and chaff were mixed for

The front of Hafod yr Abad, still a working farm, originally a Welsh long-house. *(Phil Clark)*

Right: A turnip slicer in the yard at Hafod yr Abad, the kind of equipment that would have been used. (It is now a container for growing flowers!)
(Phil Clark)

Below: The lay-shaft exposed as the building that housed the machinery is being demolished.
(Janet Handley)

animal feed), corn grinder (also for animal feed, at Trefydd Bychain there was a convenient chute from the grain store), hammer (for repair jobs) and so on. The power for this shaft came originally from a water wheel. The reservoir for this was on the slope of Cyrn y Brain opposite the farm on the other side of the road. The reservoir was called Llyn y Wolf, to scare the children away and keep them out of danger.

Above: General view of the front of Chweleiriog Goch. The date stone (1739) can be seen above the middle window. Note the lines of ornamental bricks above and below the upper windows.
(Mr Alan Moore)

Top Right: A view of the corner of the house showing the limestone foundations.
(Mr Alan Moore)

Right: The top of the gable end of an outbuilding of brick and limestone construction, with date stone (1764). *(Mr Derek Williams, Mold)*

Note that the pulleys on the shaft have no side on them to keep the belts on. Unlike modern practice with vee belts and so on, here centrifugal force kept the wide, rather loose belts between shaft and machine in position as they rotated. Later power would have come from an oil engine and then power take-off from a tractor. This equipment eventually became redundant as bagged animal feeds became readily available and there were better roads on which they could be delivered.

Chweleiriog Goch, built in 1739, is possibly the first brick built house in Llandegla parish, an area with abundant limestone available from nearby quarries. It probably acquired its name from its red brick construction to distinguish it from Chweleiriog Lwyd (grey), which is built out of limestone. (An alternative explanation depends on the colour of the soil. Around Chweleiriog Lwyd it is the usual grey colour, but there are areas of reddish soil around Chweleiriog Goch). It is likely to have been the home of some minor gentry, since its brick construction would have given the house status. The foundations are limestone, which may have been, in part at least, from an earlier building.

The bricks vary in colour, from black to red. The bricks were made locally but the remains of the kiln have unfortunately disappeared. The clay would have been fired with heather and gorse, which was common practice in rural areas before 1800, and would have accounted for the black colour of the bricks. The bricks are longer and thinner than those made today. Interestingly this house is built in the same style and at the same time as cottages in Shotwick (Cheshire).

An old will

There is much to be learnt from old documents and personal papers that have been deposited in a Record Office where they are available to any serious inquirer. Others are family keepsakes, such as the old will overleaf. The original was made suitable for study by the Hawarden Record Office, who also provided the reading below. (For future reference, do not use clear adhesive tape such as sellotape for packaging old documents – the glue soaks through and stains the document which then falls apart!)

The address on the back reads:

Mr Theo[s] Hughes of Plasnewith near Davern Dowyrch near Bwlch ruvelin near the top of the mountain near the finger post at the top of the mountain near the turnpike gate at the top of the mountain on the mountain between Wrexham and Ruthin in the County of Denbigh

The spellings are obviously as on the original document. Bwlch Rhiwfelen was a toll gate on the Horseshoe Pass, just below Pentre Bwlch (p.36).

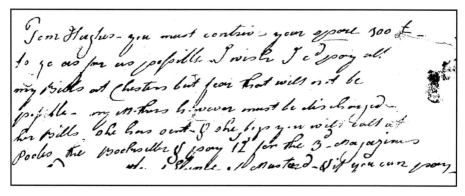

(Mrs K. Beech)

Most obedient and very humble servant till death and after death and at one side and t'other and wishing you well your wife well your little ones well and a good lock by your house this day time (but not fill'd with ale) your ob^{nt} serv^{nt} as I said before J Wms

March 14th 1797

Tom Hughes you must continue your spare £100 to go as far as possible. I wish I c^d pay all my bills at Chester but fear that will not be possible — my mother's however must be discharged — her bills she has sent & she begs you will call at Pooles the book-seller & pay 12^s for the 3^d magazines she had & a bottle of essence of mustard - & if you can pay my last years acc^t with him Hinksman I should be glad to pay — about £8 or £9 I owe him & likewise Mistress Garnons the milliner I have sent her bills & and my mother's is in it — she begs you will call upon Mrs Whitley & ask her what she owes her for a? clip bonnet she had from her — I owe Basket? about £15 but that I fear you can never pay — I have mentioned him however & if you do go to him say you only discharge that years acc^t — not any of the present year — I will send you the bills of all & then you can discharge what you can — the more the better — Barnes must be discharged — immense £25.

very late past 12 o'clock

Our supplies and services: electricity

Before Llandegla was electrified by Manweb, there were separate electricity supplies for Llandegla and Pen y Stryt. The supply of electricity for Pen y Stryt and the wiring of houses was one of T P Smith's enterprises for the Pioneer Stores (p.83). The diesel generator was housed in a small brick building that can still be seen on the slope above the Willows, though the machinery inside has now disappeared. The electricity was for lights only, and it was 'lights out' at 10.00 pm, but this must have been a great improvement over the candles and paraffin lamps that were in use then.

Mr Antur Edwards in his workshop in Llanuwchllyn. The pair of wheels in the photograph are pelton wheels. Before he started work in 1910, there was no electricity in North Wales.
(E.Curig Davies)

The original electricity supply for Llandegla village was from a generator driven by water. It is uncertain as to whether there was a pelton wheel (because of the small fall available in the water) or a turbine (because of tradition: it is still known locally as 'the turbine'). It was installed by Antur Edwards of Llanuwchllyn who specialised in such small-scale installations, particularly for farms. The concrete foundations for this can still be seen from the Offa's Dyke Path in a field just on the left past Llandegla Church, over the stile. A dam was built across the stream so that when the sluice was closed water was diverted down a leat to the turbine. This also caused water to back up under the bridge so that the mill appeared to be standing in the middle of a lake. The remains of the dam and overflow channel can be most easily seen from the new graveyard at the back of the church.

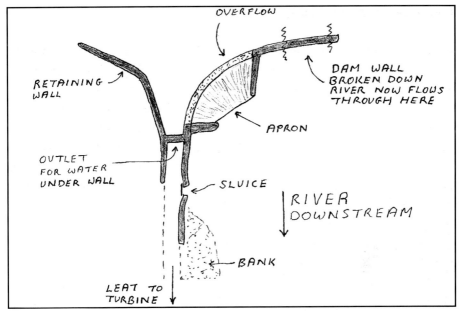

A plan to show the arrangement of walls that were built across the river to divert water to the turbine. The main sluice was in the part of the dam that is now broken down. When this was closed the water was diverted to the leat. The outlet for the water to the leat was a hole in the base of the wall, which limited the amount of water that could pass through, thus avoiding overloading the leat. An additional sluice in the side of the leat enabled water to flow back into the river. The overflow, a lower length of dam wall, allowed surplus water to return to the river.

The dam wall was sited where the river banks are steep, but when the main sluice was closed the water backed up and surrounded the mill (which would have recently closed). Away from the river, there is now no trace of the leat across the field to the turbine. (*Drawn by Phil Clark*)

The turbine was installed in the early 1930's, a performance being held in the Memorial Hall to commemorate the event. Initially there was a flicker in the light which was subsequently corrected by substituting a belt drive for the cogs between the turbine and the generator. Electricity was available from dusk until ten o'clock, three months electricity costing eleven shillings and tuppence (roughly £20 today). Neither this installation nor the one in Pen y Stryt generated enough electricity to power electric fires or cookers. In early times, the Rev J W Thomas occasionally had to leave his congregation when the lights dimmed. The church was restored to its normal brightness when he had cleared the leaves that were blocking the flow of water to the turbine. One night he fell into the river, dressed in his badminton whites, while improving the lights in the Memorial Hall.

Above: The foundations of the turbine. The water entered at this end. It left at the other end to enter the river at a bend straight ahead in the photograph. The remains of this leat are still visible along the hedgerow.
(Mrs Janet Robinson)

Left: The overflow is in the foreground. Further back is a section of the dam wall. Beyond this it is broken down allowing the river to flow unimpeded.
(Mrs Janet Robinson)

The minutes from the Parochial Church Council provide information about updating the electricity supply. In 1943 a concert was held to raise money to repair the dam, which was done in 1944. In 1948 a sub-committee was formed to make electric light available at regular times to the church and village. A new Lister generator was to be purchased to replace the turbine, which was to be sold, as was the old power house hut, which fetched £8. Regular lighting became available on May 20th 1949. In those days Bodawen was a farm. Its farm buildings were on the opposite side of the road, and it was in one of these that the new engine and generator were installed. Hywel Williams, the farmer who lived at Bodawen, Howell Edwards, who lived in the Village Cottages, and Daniel Jones volunteered to look after the new engine as well as daily starting it and then switching it off at 10.00pm every evening. They were also appointed to collect two shillings and sixpence per week per house for this amenity (£1 then would be about £18.50 today).

In May 1954 Manweb negotiated to take over Llandegla's electricity supply. £150 compensation was offered and accepted. The engine and generator were sold for £60. In 1955 Manweb provided the electricity supply for the whole village. It was supplied as a high tension supply from Ruthin to Coedpoeth. From Coedpoeth sub-station it was supplied at 11,000 volts, which was then transformed down locally.

Our supplies and services: water

Mains water came to Llandegla and Bryneglwys in 1928, and these mains have been renewed seventy-two years later early in 2000. Before this all water had to be carried from wells. Daniel Jones was paid sixpence (2$^1/_2$p) a bucket for carrying water from what is now the garden of Bryn Dŵr, near St Thomas's Mill. The wells for Pen y Stryt were behind London House: most farms had their own.

In 1930 the first flush toilets were installed in two cottages in Bryneglwys, made possible by the piped water, a considerable comfort during cold weather. As far as it is known, the Council Houses (now Maes Teg) were the first houses in Llandegla to be built (in the late 1940's) with this amenity. Before this each cottage had its own *tŷ bach*, a small shed sited at the bottom of the garden for reasons of hygiene. Inside was a horizontal board with one or more holes of an appropriate size, with a bucket under each. The bucket would be emptied on to a midden, the contents being covered with soil to spread on the fields later, or the contents buried in the garden. One former resident attributes his success with his prize-winning runner beans to the latter practice.

There was considerable drudgery associated with wash-day before mains water. The copper in the wash house had to be filled with water from the well, and a fire lit beneath to heat the water. When heated the washing and soap were added, the washing being agitated by hand with a dolly until clean. Then the whole lot was emptied by hand before another wash could be done. There was a communal wash house for the Village Cottages (p.78-80), but each of the houses opposite had their own wash house attached. The availability of running hot water made wash-day so much easier, and then washing machines came along .....

Three reservoirs, Pen Dinas, Llyn Cyfynwy and Nant y Ffridd were built towards the end of the 1800's by the Brymbo Water Company. Today they still supply water to the Brymbo and Coedpoeth area. Despite these reservoirs being in Llandegla parish, Llandegla had to wait until 1928 for its water supply from elsewhere. The original water supply for Llandegla and Bryneglwys from 1928 was untreated mountain water fed by gravity from a reservoir on the slopes of Cyrn y Brain above Hafod Bilston. The remains of the dam and some retained water can still be seen in the steep valley to the right of the first forestry road which runs right from the Offa's Dyke Path. This supply was run by the Ruthin Rural District Council. By 1947, eighty-three houses out of a total of one hundred and forty-seven in the parish were on mains water. In August 1956 the Ruthin RDC entered into an agreement with the East Denbighshire Water Company to supply water to the Llandegla area from the Pen Dinas Filter Station. The mains were laid from Pen Dinas to the village in 1957-58, along the A525 and connected up to the original cast iron pipes, so Llandegla was now supplied with treated water, still by gravity. In about 1988 the source of water was again changed. It now comes from the Alwen Reservoir, above Cerrig y Drudion, from which it needs to be pumped. Just by the Crown Hotel crossroads, behind the trees, is our water pumping station, a small building with concrete walls textured to look like brick.

Pen Dinas (and Llyn Cyfynwy) Reservoirs are fed by a leat which starts at the stream that feeds the waterfall by Trefydd Bychain and follows the contour across the slope of Cyrn y Brain through Llandegla Forest for two and a half miles. It steals water from the other streams that cross its path before it empties into Pen Dinas. This leat is still carefully maintained by the Dee Valley Water Company. It is found further uphill on the Offa's Dyke Path. If the leat is followed to the left, a little beyond

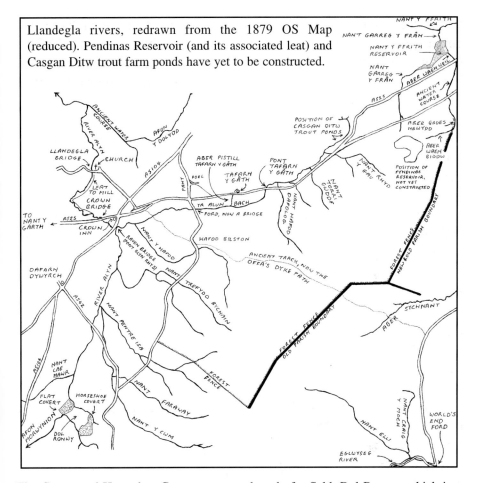

Llandegla rivers, redrawn from the 1879 OS Map (reduced). Pendinas Reservoir (and its associated leat) and Casgan Ditw trout farm ponds have yet to be constructed.

Flat Covert and Horseshoe Covert are at each end of a field, Dol Ronwy, which is a watershed. There is a small stream running down each edge. Along the northern edge is the River Alyn which flows north through Llandegla; along the southern edge is the Afon Morwynion which flows south to Bryneglwys. (A covert is a patch of dense woodland maintained to conserve game.) The cleft in the forest most easily seen from the A525 when driving from Wrexham is Nant Hafod Dafolog, where the stream flows through a steep gorge. The next valley, Nant Torri Gwddf (Breakneck Stream), describes the nature of the terrain. Several streams made part of the old parish boundary: Nant y Cwm; River Alyn; the Ancient Water Course; Aber Pistill, Tafarn y Gâth; Abergoes Newydd. The Ancient Water Course was referred to as such by John Calveley in 1812 when describing the old parish boundary which crossed Afon y Dolydd. One can surmise from this that Afon y Dolydd (which drains the valley between Fron Haul and Bodidris, and also Pant Blyddyn) was subsequently completely diverted along the Ancient Water Course. There is no trace of the original streambed to the River Alyn.

the plank bridge, one comes across an entrance to one of the original underground conduits. It is also possible to walk to the right beside the leat. Unfortunately, after some distance, unromantic but watertight plastic pipes have been laid in the leat for the rest of its length. The overflow from Pen Dinas goes into Nant y Ffridd.

There was a plan to enlarge Llyn Cyfynwy. It was then realised that the catchment area was too small for this, but not before an 'outlet tower' was built. This 'tower' is a giant raised manhole on the right-hand shore, containing valve gear that has never been used. The small building on the left as the reservoir is approached is the valve house. This is in use. Llyn Cyfynwy is a holding reservoir, water being fed by gravity from Pen

Dinas. When the water is needed during the summer it flows back to Pen Dinas filter station, which is at a lower level, by gravity assisted by pumps. The small brick hut on the left of the A5104 just after the turn to Llyn Cyfynwy, the roof of which has lost its slates, used to house the chlorination plant for Treuddyn. Llyn Cyfynwy is the largest of the three

Pen Dinas Filter Station in the early 1960's.
(Dee Valley Water Co Ltd)

reservoirs: it contains enough water to flush a modern toilet over forty-two million times. It is used as a fly fishery.

Before the car, horses were the normal means of transport and cattle were driven, not carried in lorries as today. Cattle troughs then were as important as petrol stations are now. The cattle troughs were kept topped up with water from local springs that flowed into them. Water can still be seen oozing from the banks on the left of the village hill which would have supplied the trough that used to be by the entrance to Plas Teg. That one, and one near to the bottom of The Pant, were the last two village troughs: they disappeared about twenty years ago. There was a well opposite Pentre Bwlch farm, which was filled in when the road was widened, which was also used for this purpose. (There is an excellent example of a cattle trough set into a wall on the right beside the road from Llangollen to Froncysyllte).

In days when all water had to be fetched from a well, there was an obvious limit on the amount used, so disposal of waste water was not a problem. The supply of mains water would have led to a far greater throughput of water from each house. The resulting waste water would have to go somewhere. Much of it was no doubt tipped on to the garden or down the drain, eventually finding its way into the river. Such practices would have been unacceptable with the introduction of flush toilets. For isolated buildings septic tanks would have been and are still in use. For a village such equipment is unsuitable as there is insufficient area for the treated effluent to percolate into the soil. In 1957 a sewage works was constructed on the left of the Offa's Dyke Path just near Llandegla Church. In 1969 the existing sewage works opposite the Crown Hotel were built, the original sewage works being converted into a pumping station. The effluent flows by gravity to the old sewage works, is pumped uphill to the crest of the village hill and then again flows by gravity to the new sewage works. Though much larger than the original one, the capacity of the new works is still a factor to be taken into account when considering the number of new houses that could be built in Llandegla.

Things now gone

The most significant building that has now gone is **St Thomas's Mill**. It is thought that milling was carried out on this site from the sixteenth century, but not in the mill illustrated. This mill worked until the early 1920's and was demolished in the 1950's. It is known that Robert Jones was miller at least between the years 1894 and 1895. The gentleman in the lower photograph named William Davies was the miller in 1898, the date of these photographs. He was the last miller and he also mended

A view of the end of St Thomas's Mill, looking up to the centre of the village. The building in the left foreground was used by the miller for storing bags of grain and flour. The cottage just behind the mill is Bryn Dŵr, where the miller lived. Behind this Mill Farm (now Mill Cottage) and the end of Church Terrace can be seen. The Hand is further back on the left, the outline of the church can be distinguished behind the trees. This water wheel is an overshot wheel: the water is carried over the wheel by the leat.

Llandegla Village, Part of (snow on the ground) 1898

Llandegla Mill, River Alyn & Bridge (snow on the ground)

The other end of the Mill. The bridge in the background over the River Alyn carries the road from the village. This water wheel is a pitch-back wheel: the water leaves the wheel on the same side as the leat. Because of this arrangement the water wheels rotate in opposite directions to each other. *(Mr Tegla Jones)*

shoes. Times were hard and it was not unusual for men to take on other work to make ends meet. He died in 1924 age 74. He is buried at the mill end of the churchyard, at his request, to keep an eye on his property. His grave can still be visited.

The Old Mill, Llandegla

A photograph of the Mill taken at a later date. It is now in a poor state of repair, the leat has disappeared. *(Mr Tegla Jones)*

A view of the bridge. The storage building can still be seen on the right, with Bryn Dŵr behind. The path to the right before the bridge is where cattle were led down to drink from the river.
(Mr Tegla Jones)

The same view a little later.
(Mr Tegla Jones)

Now Bryn Dŵr stands on its own. Both the Mill and the storage building have gone, there is garden where they once stood.
(Janet Handley)

However, this was just one of the many water mills up and down the country that fall into disuse and are eventually demolished or converted to other uses. Other losses seem to be the result of an urge to tidy up. Planning permission was given for a new farm house to be built at **Tomen y Rhodwydd Farm** provided that the old one, which would have been of historical interest but unlisted, was demolished and all rubble taken away from the site. The new house at Tomen y Rhodwydd Farm is an attractive residence but without historical interest.

A general view of Tomen y Rhodwydd Farm in 1998, just before demolition
(Mr E.Owen)

Formerly aggrandisement was achieved by building the new house on to an existing structure, as was done at the Old Rectory and Hafod Bilston. Here the new buildings were built onto the end of the old ones, the

Detail of the house. The original stone walls have been rendered. *(Mr E.Owen)*

accommodation being combined internally. On the other hand there were instances where the old building was taken down and the old foundations reused, as at Chweleiriog Goch. Building techniques have since changed, which may preclude this kind of reuse today.

Obtaining planning permission is usually straightforward if a house is to be replaced to provide a modern standard of comfort when the owner needs to live on site, as for a farm. The aim of this procedure is to avoid an increase in the number of houses dotted around the countryside by stealth. Two points arise. Firstly, vigilance is needed: if there is concern about a threat to a building of potential historical interest the local conservation officer can make an assessment and CADW can spot list, if appropriate. Secondly, in former times the skills needed to bring a Welsh longhouse up to a then acceptable standard at a reasonable cost would have been commonplace. Now the restoration of an old building is specialist work. This, together with today's expectation of comfort, make the restoration of an old building as a dwelling very expensive. Costs are also involved if an old building is to be mothballed. Despite the problems, efforts should be made to see if it is possible to keep these bits of our history for future generations. When a building has been pulled down its history goes as well.

The Llandegla tram

Tram No.78 was the last new tram delivered in 1920 to the Wallasey Corporation tramways, costing over £2000. The Wallasey system closed in 1933, the last trams being sold off for £5 to £10 each to a very uncertain future. Tram No. 78 became an agricultural building on Rhos

Isa farm, without its upper deck and the ends where the driver stood. It was used for the storage of grain during the last war.

In 1985 rescue came. It was loaded on to a lorry and moved to Liverpool then to Birkenhead where

(Both from the Alf Jacob Photographic Collection with permission from the Merseyside Tram Preservation Society)

The lower saloon jacked up ready for a flat bed lorry to move under neath.

restoration started - but only for about a year. In 1997 with the help of a £36,000 Heritage Lottery grant restoration was restarted. Now at the end of 2001, after a total of £45.000 and many thousands of volunteer manhours, it is ready to take to the rails again. The driving ends have been rebuilt, the upper deck, found in Shropshire, has been put back. Missing timbers have been painstakingly copied from surviving woodwork (fortunately this was rot-resistant teak). Small original details are back *in situ*, such as lines of brass match plates along the windowsills for striking matches (there was a different attitude to smoking then!) and "Do not spit on the

Getting ready for the move: Mr William Owen looks out of the door, with Medwyn Owen on his left. Others are from the Merseyside Tram Preservation Society.

tram" notices. This beautifully restored tram is as near as possible to its condition when delivered new in 1920. Hopefully it will be in service in 2002 on the Birkenhead Heritage Tramway.

Restored Tram No. 78. The design was regarded as old fashioned even in 1920, but it is appropriate for the area, the seaside resort of New Brighton. The sea air can be appreciated from the balcony seats!
(Medwyn Owen)

7. LLANDEGLA OUT OF DOORS

Perhaps the best way to enjoy exploring the history of this beautiful area is on foot, taking advantage of one of the many public footpaths to spot historical landmarks and enjoy the scenery at the same time. Here are some suggestions for places to visit and paths to follow.

The Ponderosa and the radio masts

Our nearest famous beauty spot, the Horseshoe Pass, attracts visitors from far afield. For around the last seventy years the **Ponderosa Café** at the head of the Pass has looked after their bodily needs, providing refreshment in the middle of incomparable scenery. Mr Hill, who lived at Plas Norway, ran the Café until the Second World War, when it was closed. By the end of the war it was derelict. Soon after Mr David Williams built a new café which is now at the centre of the existing complex. He was known locally as 'Dai the Mule' as this was the form of transport used - he had to collect all of his water from St Collen's Well (p.17). Not only had the water to be carried about a quarter of a mile, but much of it was up a steep slope, so no doubt he was most grateful for the efforts of the mule. Water is now pumped from a private spring and passes through a modern treatment plant before use.

After two further changes of ownership, the Clemences acquired the café in 1982 and the business has steadily developed. If you visit it is worth looking at the timbers in the dining area. They came from a Cheshire barn, but were originally ship's timbers, thought to be 16th century. Being in such a popular spot, it sees the best and worst of life. The café has been host to many well known stars of sport and television, including the Dutch National Football Team. The downside has included a murder, a number of suicide attempts (some successful) and several fatal road accidents in the last twenty years.

The name 'Ponderosa'? It was the ranch in the popular 1960's television series *Bonanza*.

The Ponderosa Café in about 1935-36. **From left to right**: Miss Maggie Roberts (later Bolton), Pentre Dŵr; Mr Harry Drakeley, Pentre Dŵr; Miss Evelyn Davies, Tai Newyddion; Mr Frederick Hill, owner. *(Mr John Clemence)*

Now in a rather dilapidated state, the Café in about 1952. *(Mr John Clemence)*

An aerial view of the Ponderosa in 1998, much expanded to cope with the popularity of the Horseshoe Pass with tourists. The A542 to Llangollen runs from upper right to lower left. The road to Pentre Dŵr leaves the A542 to the right behind the Ponderosa. The road at the top skirts the slate tips to become a single track road to Bryneglwys. From the Llangollen end of the car park extends the trackbed of the tramway which was used to transport slate from the Moel y Faen quarry, now a level and attractive walk. In places the positions of the sleepers are still just visible in the grass.
(Reproduced with permission from Mr R.P.Jones, Dragon Aviation, Wrexham)

There are three masts on the hill, Cyrn y Brain, that rises up from the back of the Ponderosa. These masts belong to the BBC, British Telecom, and are used by the Ambulance Service, British Gas and other organisations that require long distance communications. It is not possible to drive up to the masts as there is a locked gate at the bottom of the track. The lock is an amazing contraption, with eight padlocks. Pedestrian access can be gained by a stile at the back of the Ponderosa.

On the way up to the masts on the right are the brick and concrete foundations of the wartime radar masts (p.64). After the war, these masts were cut up to make fence posts, which are still scattered about. The row of insulators on each one distinguishes them from ordinary fence posts. It is a stiff walk up to the masts, but well worth it because of the breathtaking views. There is a cairn to the left of the track opposite the first mast, which seems to have been modified for use as a barbecue. Further to the west there is another cairn, a low mound covered with heather. Looking ahead the mound on the left of the third mast is Sir Watkin's Tower. As you walk on, the corner of the Forest fence is reached, partly supported by a piece of radar mast (p.8). After the third mast the track deteriorates, but it is worth persisting. There is a

stile at a slight bend in the fence line. 'PU' is inscribed on the slab beneath the stile: it is an old boundary stone which would have been set vertically. The fence line is not only the edge of Llandegla Forest (p.136), it is also the old parish boundary (p.7) and the border of a Poor Law Union (p.40), hence 'PU'.

The old boundary stone that lies on the ground under the stile on the way to Sir Watkin's Tower *(Phil Clark)*

Over this stile the narrow path soon reaches a trig point. The grass-covered pile of rocks adjacent to this is the remains of Sir Watkin's Tower. A proud landowner, he is reputed to have used his tower to view his properties in seven counties. He chose his spot well: if you look about while standing on this pile of rocks on a clear day, the view is just spectacular.

Returning to the stile, further along the fence on the other side, is a leaning boundary stone. Eventually a ladder stile is reached at *Y Ddwy Garreg Henben* (The Two Old Top Rocks). This is the Offa's Dyke Path, about two and a half miles from the Ponderosa.

The Offa's Dyke Path

Walkers have tramped the six miles of the Offa's Dyke Path that passes through our parish since the path was opened in 1971. Offa's Dyke itself was built as a defensive earthwork in the eighth century. It runs about six miles east of Llandegla and Treuddyn seems to be its northernmost point. The original idea was for the path to follow the Dyke as closely as possible. Where this was not practicable, for example due to urban development, a route was chosen for its scenic quality. This is why it passes through Llandegla.

As roughly two thirds of walkers pass from south to north, this is how we will note the features of Llandegla that can be seen from the path. At World's End there is a ford. As soon as you cross this you are in the Parish of Llandegla. Just before the ford, a brief diversion can be made to look at the stream along the track to the left. Soon the fully fledged stream (the River Eglwyseg) can be seen emerging from a spoil heap. Above the spoil heap there is the mine entrance from which it came. Lead and silver were mined here. (The other 'mine entrance' on the right of the path is possibly a natural cavern). Further up the road from World's End there is another spoil heap in the valley on the left. These are remnants of what was a very busy industrial area in the eighteenth and nineteenth centuries, particularly further up the road and to the right towards Minera.

As you start up the path away from the road, marked by the acorn waymark, a looming mass of conifers can be seen on the horizon. This bank of sitka spruce is the upper edge of Llandegla Forest (p.136). The ragged trees to the left of this are lodgepole pine. The radio masts are on Cyrn y Brain (p.129). A boardwalk, made from old railway sleepers, forms part of the path to the forest (once heather has been broken down by regular trampling it does not easily regenerate, in contrast to the green meadows on the other side of Llandegla). Halfway to the forest, the path crosses Aber Sychnant, whose waters eventually enter the River Dee via Wrexham.

131

All of this path, up to and through the forest to Hafod Bilston, is an old track. The ladder stile that gains access to the Forest is at Y Ddwy Garreg Henben. The fence marks an old parish boundary (p.7), so this fence line is probably ancient. Shortly after entering the forest there is a forest road that comes in from the right. This is part of an old road (Glasfryn Road) that used to link the quarries of the Horseshoe Pass with the industrial area around Minera, very active in the eighteenth century. It would have been at this point that the old track (now the Offa's Dyke Path) and Glasfryn Road would have crossed: *Croes Degla* (Tecla's Cross) (p.7). Glasfryn Road to the west of Croes Degla has disappeared. Instead of crossing the ladder stile, it is possible to follow the fence to the left, past the radio masts and then down the track to the Ponderosa Café. To the right it is not suitable for walking. Pen Dinas Reservoir can be reached via the Glasfryn Road or a forestry road (p.117).

In the forest, part of the way down the steep slope, the path crosses and runs beside a leat (p.117). In it the clear mountain water flows towards Pen Dinas Reservoir, to be drunk later by the inhabitants of Brymbo and Coedpoeth. Where the leat and the path run together they cross the bottom of a ride. This is one of two rides, each of which is about half a mile long. The rides have been made by felling trees to provide long lengths of woodland edge which are particularly valuable for wildlife conservation (p.138). Further down a forestry road crosses the path. If you turn right on this, after a short distance the remains of a dam and reservoir can be seen to the left down a steep valley. This was Llandegla's water supply for over twenty years (p.117).

A little lower down on the left of the path, a vertical multi-coloured pipe marks the site of the Hafod Hwntw Lead Mine. It does not seem to have been a very successful operation, it was only active for about four years from 1907. There were numerous complaints from Hafod Bilston, whose water supply came from a short distance downstream, that their water was being contaminated with lead from the workings. Complaints were also made about the effect of the mine on sport, presumably the grouse shoot. The proprietors came from south Glamorgan hence the name (*hwntw* is a North Wales term for someone who comes from South Wales).

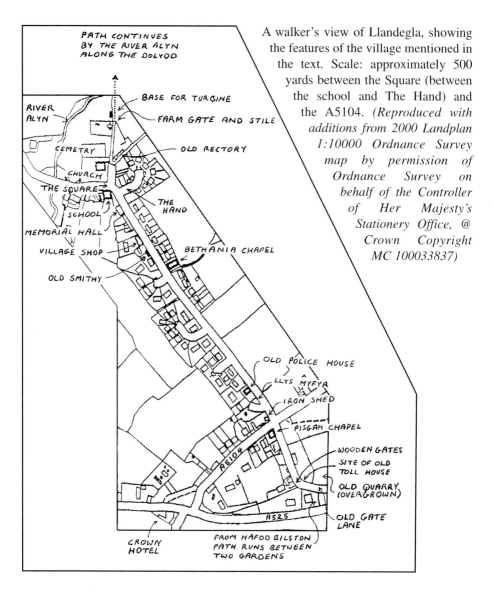

A walker's view of Llandegla, showing the features of the village mentioned in the text. Scale: approximately 500 yards between the Square (between the school and The Hand) and the A5104. *(Reproduced with additions from 2000 Landplan 1:10000 Ordnance Survey map by permission of Ordnance Survey on behalf of the Controller of Her Majesty's Stationery Office, @ Crown Copyright MC 100033837)*

At the bottom of the slope the path passes through the hamlet of Hafod Bilston. From Hafod Bilston it crosses fields and the A525, goes up a short passage between two gardens and then you arrive at Old Gate Lane. Inside the bend in the lane is the site of an old toll house, now covered by tarmac, which gave the lane its name (p.38). The private drive behind tall wooden gates on the left used to be the road to the

Crown Hotel and Ruthin, before the section of the A525 which you have just crossed was built (p.38). The house next door has a plaque on the wall: it was the home of Tegla Davies (pp.190-191). The chapel on the left at the crossroads is Pisgah Chapel (p.186), the house opposite is London House (pp.80-83). Just over the crossroads is a large iron shed which used to house the village bus (which it fitted like a glove). Coal was once sold from here.

Continuing down the road towards the centre of the village, the red brick house on the left is Llys Myfyr (Court of Studying), built as a manse in 1924 for the minister of Bethania Chapel. It was also where other ministers came to study, hence the name. The minister had seven children, so it must have been quite a crowd on occasion! Its garage is rather small as it was built just large enough to house a motorcycle and sidecar. The square house next door to Llys Myfyr was built as a police house for the local bobby in 1938, but has been a private house since 1993. The half-timbered house on the right, Plas Rhyd, is modern. Plas Rhyd means Ford Place: nothing to do with crossing water, Ford was the surname of the builder! Bethania Chapel (p.185) is the red brick chapel on the right: both this and Pisgah are in regular use. Next on the left comes White Horse Cottage, which used to be a drovers' pub (p.89); the Old Smithy (pp.46, 80); Bro Tegla, set back from the road on the site of the old Smithy yard; the Village Shop and Cottages which also housed a drovers' pub (pp.78, 91); and the Memorial Hall (p.209).

Ahead to the right of the bridge is the Alyn Park and Picnic Area (pp.141-142) - a peaceful place to rest the feet beside a cooling stream. The Offa's Dyke Path turns right opposite the school (pp.158-180) between Llandegla Church (pp.181-185) and the Hand (p.91). The Hand was formerly an inn but is now a private house, which breaks a tradition: village pubs are often located by the village church. When a church was under construction, master craftsmen would have been employed from elsewhere who would have needed accommodation, hence the presence of an inn. The Hand, like many pubs in the old days, used to be a working farm also: the terrace of cottages next door, Trem yr Eglwys, has recently been converted from an old shippon.

The path passes the Old Rectory (p.73) on the right and then the former sewage works on the left (p.120). The meadows on the right (the *Dolydd*) are where the drovers used to stable their cattle overnight: there was access to both grass and water (p.31). Over the stile the concrete base for the 'turbine' (p.114) can be seen on the left. By here is a short section of an old road, marked by a double row of thorn trees. The path follows and then crosses the River Alyn, then follows further sections of the old road, much of it a water-filled ditch bounded by single or double rows of trees. (The River Alyn follows a circuitous course: it flows north around Mold, then south down to Wrexham before going east into the Dee.)

Eventually with double farmgates ahead, the path turns left down a dry part of the old road, this part being *Ffordd y Saint* (The Saints' Road). From here until the cattle grid on the other side of the B5431 you are following the parish boundary along Ffordd y Saint: Llanarmon yn Iâl on the right, Llandegla on the left. Where the path crosses the B5431 is known locally as Saints' Crossing. Evidence on the ground and from old

Saints' Road looking towards Llandegla. The hedgerow on the left is in Llanarmon parish, that on the right is in Llandegla parish. The Offa's Dyke Path continues along this before turning sharp right before the river Alyn. The remains of single and double rows of trees indicating the route of the old road from here to Llandegla village can be seen from the Path. *(Janet Handley)*

maps suggests that all of these old roads were one, which would have run from St Tecla's Well to St Garmon's, hence Ffordd y Saint. Just before Saints' Crossing is the region in which neolithic remains have been found in limestone caves (p.11). St Garmon's Well is sited in the field bounded by the green railings by Saints' Crossing (p.18).

At Saints' Crossing there is a stone name plaque for Chweleiriog Lwyd. Chweleiriog was the old name for the township that used to be in the present parishes of Llanarman yn Iâl and Llandegla (p.24), it is now just the name for two farms. From the cattle grid, Chweleiriog Lwyd is the square grey farm house that lies straight ahead. To the left in the distance part of Chweleiriog Goch (p.110) can just be discerned among the trees. Just beyond the cattle grid the parish boundary follows a hedgerow accompanied by a very small stream, curving away to the left. The path swings right following the road. As you follow this you are leaving the Parish of Llandegla: safe journey!

Coed Llandegla (Llandegla Forest)

Approaching Llandegla from Wrexham, the hillside on the left is covered with conifers. This is Llandegla Forest, covering over sixteen thousand acres. The following information is compiled from the Tilhill Economic Forestry Management and Design Plan, 2000-2010. The timber from the forest goes to Shotton Paper Mill for the manufacture of paper. Most of the trees are sitka spruce, but ten percent are larch. These are on a slope facing the A525 and are a feature in the autumn when the leaves change colour. The cutting of the larch here is done in such a way that a continuous cover is maintained, so avoiding any bare patches.

The forest was planted in 1971-72, which means that all of the trees are about the same age. Trees are normally harvested when they are forty years old, so these would be ready for felling in 2011-12. Tilhill Economic Forestry, who manage the Forest, will be restructuring the forest. Rather than clear felling large areas, it is intended in future to fell the trees in small areas, which will greatly reduce the visual impact.

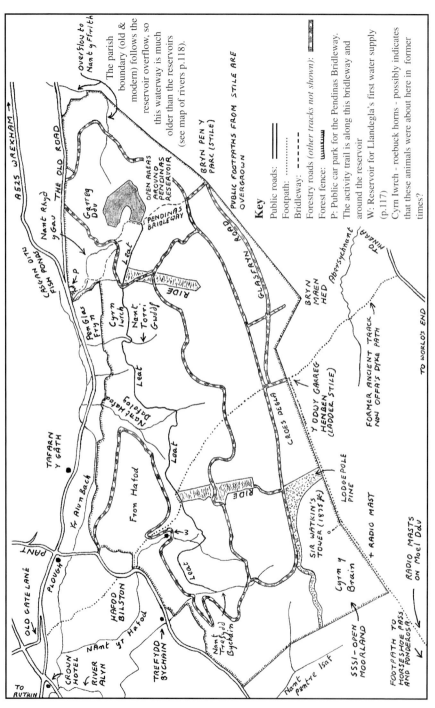

The parish boundary (old & modern) follows the reservoir overflow, so this waterway is much older than the reservoirs (see map of rivers p.118).

Key

Public roads:
Footpath:
Bridleway:
Forestry roads (*other tracks not shown*):
Forest fence:
P: Public car park for the Pendinas Bridleway.
The activity trail is along this bridleway and around the reservoir
W: Reservoir for Llandegla's first water supply (p.117)
Cym Iwrch – roebuck horns – possibly indicates that these animals were about here in former times?

PUBLIC FOOTPATHS FROM STILE ARE OVERGROWN

Llandegla Forest (*redrawn with permission from The Ordnance Survey and Tilhill Economic Forestry*)

137

This strategy is helped by the uneven growth of trees due to the variable terrain. By harvesting some trees early and others late, eventually the forest will be made up of trees of different ages. This restructuring will take twenty to thirty years to complete. The forest will then become continuously productive and will also provide an improved habitat for wildlife.

Areas of open ground are maintained, particularly in the vicinity of Pen Dinas Reservoir. In these, rowan (mountain ash) and other bushes are starting to grow. The heather in the open areas is cut in rotation as the new growth is more nutritious than the old. Two heather rides, each about half a mile long, have been cut through the forest. As the forest is restructured, these open rides, and a few of the stream gullies (some of these are being kept untouched), will be connected with the open moorland at the top of Cyrn y Brain to provide wildlife corridors. Deadwood will be allowed to remain in certain areas where it is not a danger: rotting timber is valuable for maintaining species diversity in woodland. Other conservation measures include brashing (cutting off the branches of conifers to about head height) alongside roads, streamside clearance, heather flailing and bracken spraying. These measures will enhance the forest edge effect, providing a preferred habitat for much wildlife, in particular our local population of black grouse, a bird that has become uncommon.

Roughly a third of the forest is a catchment area for water supplies (the average rainfall is 44.3 inches). Care is taken while felling trees near to water courses as sudden removal of tree cover can easily upset the quality of the water. It is normal forestry practice to treat tree stumps with urea in order to avoid parasitic fungi spreading from the tree stumps to healthy trees. Though not very poisonous in itself, and completely biodegradable, urea could increase the nitrate in the water, so it is not used within three hundred yards of a water course.

The forest is open for the general public to wander in (though some paths may be closed one day a year for legal reasons), on foot or mountain bike but not on any powered means of transport. There are nine miles of well-built forestry roads and sixteen miles of track which provide easy walking, and further lengths of footpaths, but beware of forestry traffic. The Offa's Dyke Path (p.131) passes through it. There is a popular bridleway (and car parking facilities) up to Pen Dinas Reservoir, complete with a fitness trail. This has seven items of timber-built physical exercise equipment for those who have energy to burn during the steep walk up. The fishing rights to Pen Dinas reservoir are owned by the Shotton Fly-Fishing Club. The sporting rights are owned by the Tilhill Economic Forestry but are not active.

Llandegla's weather station

A weather station used to be sited behind the trig point on the hill above Llyn Cyfynwy. There is now nothing left, except for the level area just behind the trig point which marks the site (it is still labelled as 'Meteorological Station' on the OS Explorer Map, published in summer 2000!). It is rewarding to walk up to the site to enjoy the extensive view from the top (but check with the Fish Farm first).Construction started in 1969, it operated from the summer of 1971 and was demolished after four years of use. As part of the Agreement with the Bodidris Estate who owned the land, all remains, including the heavy concrete base to the tower, were to be removed and the site returned as far as possible to its original state. The Barritts of Bodidris were most concerned that the natural beauty would not be permanently spoilt.

This short-lived research station was part of the Dee Weather Radar Project. It was a cooperative scheme jointly sponsored by the Meteorological Office, the Water Resources Board (now part of the Department of the Environment) and Plessey Radar, who provided the equipment. The Dee Valley Catchment Area was chosen as there was already some on-going research into river regulation by means of regulating reservoirs. The site at 1300ft (350m) near Llyn Cyfynwy was chosen as it was from there that the radar could 'see' over the catchment area.

The aim was to develop a radar system that could measure the quantity of rainfall as it was falling in order to provide immediate information for water management and river regulation. To do this measurements were made to find the relationship between the amount of rain and the ability of it to reflect a radar beam before it reached the ground. A meter to measure the sizes of raindrops (a distrometer) was used as there is a relationship between the sizes of the drops, the rainfall and the reflection of the radar.

Around seventy self-reading gauges were spread over the River Dee Catchment Area, roughly around Llangollen, Corwen, Bala and the Alwen Reservoir. There were none in our parish. Unlike the conventional rain gauges that just fill up with water, these measured the water as it passed through the gauge. Each gauge contained its own

The tower of the weather station was 6m (20 feet) high. It carried a scanner, an anemometer and a radio for remotely reading the rain gauges that could be interrogated. The buildings contained an operations room, transmitter room, workshop, office and living accommodation. *(Plessey Radar)*

miniature tape recorder, so it could remain in place for up to several months before the measurements were recovered. Some were equipped in such a way that they could be interrogated by radio from the tower while the reflection of the radar was also being measured.

The present-day use of radar for measuring rainfall was founded on this project. The project also provided information about the pattern of rainfall and the influence of the lie of the land on this, to help water management in the Dee Valley Catchment Area.

There was a second weather station by Pen Dinas Reservoir. This was a group of meteorological instruments that were assembled by Grove Park School, Wrexham. For forty years they were read regularly for the school by Maldwyn Evans.

Alyn Park and Picnic Area

This is an area of common land for the use of residents of Llandegla and visitors to the village. It is on both sides of the River Alyn, to the right of the bridge. Here (*Hen Gwarchae*) local stray livestock were kept until claimed. In more recent years it was used as a rubbish tip by the village. In 1986, at the instigation of Ken Bellis, the then Chair of the Community Council, the surface rubbish was removed and a layer of soil

was spread over the former tip to keep the contents safely buried. Trees were

The volunteers pictured here are Jill Clark, Susan Percival, Mike Byrne, Dr Bickford and Jim Ashworth.

(Reproduced with permission from Graham Catherall Photography, Connah's Quay)

planted. It is now a leafy glade. Alyn Park and the bridge over the stream are also the resting place of an exorcised ghost (p.77).

In 1983, the Community Council decided to reclaim the site with the aid of the Youth Training Scheme and in 1984, a working party of local residents was formed to transform and maintain the area. In July 1986, the work of the villagers was brought to the attention of the Council for the Protection of Rural Wales (CPRW) and an award was presented at the Royal Welsh Show, Builth Wells. Since then, the area has won a number of awards: in 1992, a certificate of merit in the Wales in Bloom Competition and in 1995, equal third prize in the environmental section of a competition run by Clwyd Voluntary Services Council. The area is now maintained by a group of volunteers and is well used by the community and visitors to the village: a welcome haven for walkers after the rigours of trudging along the Offa's Dyke Path.

Steps leading down from the road to the river Alyn. Saint Tecla's Church is in the background.
(Miss Fleur Davies)

The stepping stones across a babbling brook (the River Alyn!)   *(Mrs Sheila Byrne)*

A view under the bridge from Alyn Park. The bole of the tree by the bridge is the one important to the Old Rectory ghost (p.77).   *(Mrs Sheila Byrne)*

The great snows

Before we leave the reader to enjoy these rambles, it is as well to remember that extreme weather conditions can occur in this region! The

The 1963 snow: a view of the AA box, and an AA motorcycle and sidecar, near to the (then) new roundabout at Dafarn Dyrwych. This will revive memories for some motorists as the motorcycle and sidecars were being phased out in the early 1960's to be replaced by mini vans. (There are still twenty-two AA boxes existing in the UK, four in Wales, which are now listed as structures of historical interest). *(Haydn Edwards)*

Another view of the snow by the Dafarn Dyrwych roundabout. It was so deep that it reached the top of the signposts, one of which is forming an unusual perch for David and Gareth Davies and Haydn Edwards.
(Haydn Edwards)

Here the villagers are clearing the Village Hill, which was completely blocked.
(Haydn Edwards)

144

snows of the winter of 1963 are still remembered, when the village was snowed in for three to four days. Hywel Williams of Bodawen Farm (pp.77, 115) had permission from the Milk Marketing Board to sell milk. Each customer had to bring their own jug. Bread was also a problem. Greatorex's van came as far as it could from Bwlchgwyn to meet customers from Llandegla who had walked over the moors through the snow. The 1947 snows were even worse and much deeper. Many hundreds of sheep were buried alive and Forestry Commission horses perished through lack of food.

8. THE ESTATES

Much of Llandegla was owned and dominated by the Bodidris estate, but other estates such as Accre Hall and Hafod Bilston also owned land in the parish. Though the paternalistic influence that these houses once exerted has now gone the houses are still here.

Hafod Bilston (*Dr John Bickford*)

Hafod Bilston is a decidedly unusual house, being a three-storey building with stone mullioned windows in what seems to be a relatively remote situation. It is clear that it must have been altered substantially at various points in its history and the fact that it was not separated from the actual hillside above it by any substantial ditch until about 1944 must have made for a very damp interior. The position of the door on the side of the house most exposed to wind and rain must also have been a considerable disadvantage. Whether there was an entry lobby is not clear but there would not seem to have been much space for one. It is possible that the rear portion of the house was originally a Welsh 'long house'.

Hafod Bilston: formerly at the centre of a farm, now just a private dwelling. Note the mullioned windows.
(*Janet Handley*)

The main portion of the house is elegant, with four-paned stone mullioned windows on

146

Most of the farm buildings have now been given over to other uses. This one has been thoughtfully converted into a dwelling. *(Janet Handley)*

each floor. The chimney is at the side of the house and this suggests that the design was that of a small "hall house" with a large fireplace heating the main part of the building. It has been suggested that what is now the window of the first floor may have been a very important feature of the lighting of the building. Another striking feature is the large stone lintel over the now blocked-in doorway. These features suggest that the date of the building was sometime about 1600, perhaps later rather than earlier.

Whether the house was originally built as a hunting lodge is debatable, but it certainly later became a farm and underwent considerable modification in the process. A large bread oven is still a conspicuous feature of the kitchen and it appears that the top floor was used largely as a grain store with a hoist to a window at the rear end of the house: a mass of grain had collected between the irregular floor-boards. The timber beams supporting the roof are massive and it seems a pity that the details of the woodwork have been largely obscured by paint in more recent times.

It is evident that compared with its original elegant if rather small beginnings, Hafod Bilston underwent many changes and in the end became almost redundant when modern farming methods resulted in the amalgamation of three small farms, Trefydd Bychain, Hafod Bilston and

Llyn Rhys, into one unit. As a result the house had been unoccupied for several years before 1970, by which time former townspeople found it possible and desirable to live "in the country". By 1970 the floor timbers were quite irregular and in places distinctly sloping. Several unusually shaped bedrooms had their own quaint charm in spite of their inconvenience. There was at that time only an outside toilet and no bathroom as such. The basically elegant frontage had been defaced by a rather crude cement wash. This was removed to reveal the original stonework and to allow it to be re-pointed.

An aerial view of Hafod Bilston in 1971. There are open fields at the back: this photograph would have been taken in the summer just before the planting of Llandegla Forest started. The three blocks of farm buildings around the house have all been converted into dwellings, the one with the pig sty in front of the yard is shown above. The Offa's Dyke Path now roughly follows the field boundary as it slopes on the right. *(Reproduced with permission from Mr. R. P. Jones, Dragon Aviation, Wrexham)*

The precise history of Hafod Bilston does not seem to have been recorded. The name 'Bilston' is a local variation on the family name 'Puleston' and we are indebted to the late Mrs Sunter Harrison of Wrexham for much detailed information about this family. The Puleston family were already living in Emral Hall near Worthenbury in 1284. They were in possession of this property until 1936 and the Hall has since been demolished. They were an influential family with social and political connections over a great part of North Wales and especially in the Wrexham area and the Vale of Clwyd. A John Puleston, born in 1580, lived in a house rather curiously named *Pwll yr Uwd* (The Porridge Pool) on the Holt side of Wrexham and his second son came to live in Llandegla. His will, dated 1668, has been preserved and he describes himself as 'John Puleston, of Treby Buchan in ye County of Denbigh, gent.'. We cannot say positively that he was the owner of Hafod Bilston, but it is at least possible, the house being in the ancient township of Trefydd Bychain.

The name of the house has varied over the years. It is probably the house mentioned as *Yr Hafod* by Humphrey Llwyd in his *Parochalia* of 1695-98. The other houses named as being in 'Llan Dekla' are *Y Bwych bychan, Llethy'r Lhygoden, Tŷ y Graig* and *Hafod Davoleg* (original spellings). It is referred to as 'Hafod Bulston' in a document of 1830 and both as 'Havod Puleston' and 'Hafod Bilston' in 1847. Interestingly enough Peter Smith in his monumental work of 1975, *Houses of the Welsh Countryside*, calls the house 'Hafoty Puleston', and local speech still retains the intermediate 'y'.

The Bodidris Estate

Bodidris lies about two miles from the village of Llandegla down a hedge-lined country lane off the A5104 road towards Chester. It is a spectacular stone building clothed by ivy, standing in its own grounds. Visiting the house today, one can still see parts of its colourful past. The original house, believed to have been of 'keep' shape, has been traced back to 1311. It was rebuilt in 1550, in Tudor times, and the ancient

Bodidris
*(Janet
Handley)*

house now standing shows a strong Tudor influence. It has a prison cell, priesthole and duelling staircase. There are mullioned windows, hoodmoulds, heraldic and decorative finials and a cyclopean lintel. Situated in an oak panel behind the bar is the shield showing the coat of arms of the Lloyd family of Bodidris. In the Tudor Room there is a decorative candelabrum with the sanctuary ring which is thought to have come from Valle Crucis Abbey.

Outside there is an arched gothic doorway, possibly originating from Valle Crucis Abbey. A friendly lion of unknown origin greets you while the 'manor stone of Bodidris' stands in the ground below. The Earl of

The Tudor
Room,
Bodidris
*(Janet
Handley)*

Leicester's crest, the Bear and Ragged Staff, is visible on the front gable of the Hall. There is a saracen's head on the front of the end of the stable gable. The clock that was claimed from the school is sited in the

tower of the stable block. Mrs Eileen Clarke, whose husband was chauffeur at Bodidris, remembers, "Bodidris had its own time, twenty minutes faster than the village. I am not sure why, except it was apparently an old custom, perhaps so that they were never late for anything." The large mounting block remains in the courtyard, marking the original boundary between Denbighshire and Flintshire.

Left: The garden at Bodidris, as pictured on a postcard from between the two World Wars, when there were adequate resources for its maintenance. *(Mr Tegla Jones)*

Right: The boundary stone in Bodidris car park. The boundary goes left from the stone through the Hall wall, and straight ahead at a right angle (see map on p.6). The former stable block is on the right and beautiful Denbighshire in the winter sun in the distance. *(Phil Clark)*

Left: A face-view of the stone. It is approximately $3\frac{1}{2}$ feet long by $2\frac{1}{2}$ feet high *(Phil Clark)*

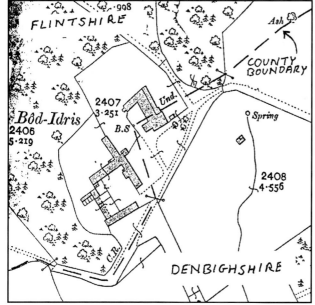

A map of Bodidris taken from the 1912 OS map. The county boundary (p.22) passed through Bodidris just as one entered the dining room. Each field is numbered with its size in acres. The ash tree has now gone: such trees were often used as waymarks for boundaries but even ash trees have a limited life!

Und: Boundary undefined on the ground
CR: Boundary down centre of the road (soon after it follows a small stream)
BS: Boundary stone

The following account of the history of Bodidris is a synopsis of 'Bodidris Llandegla', a well illustrated and detailed history of Bodidris published by four members of the Llandegla Womens' Institute, Janet Handley, Janet Robinson, Edna Oulton and Norma Bird. This book, together with additional information and illustrations, can be seen in the Ruthin Record Office (Denbighshire County Council).

Its owners and their circumstances have been varied. From its early origins to 1843, inheritance secured ownership. The original hereditary owners were the famous Lloyd family, who lived in Bodidris for a total of over five hundred years with thirteen family exchanges down the line. The first Lloyd, who built the house and gave his brother Idris's name to Bodidris, was Gruffudd ap Llewelyn, married to Tagwystyl whose sepulchral slab is situated in St Tysilio Parish Church, Bryneglwys. It is possible that this slab was transferred from Valle Crucis Abbey about the year 1400. The mailed effigy of Gryffudd ap Llewellyn, who was disembowelled by his sword, can be seen in St Garmon's church, Llanarmon yn Iâl. A picture of his fate used to hang in Bodidris, but it was recently removed as it rather put the guests off their dinner!

Another notable Lloyd was John, the fourth child of David and Mallt Lloyd. He was Abbot of Valle Crucis Abbey and may have been responsible for the two chandeliers which now hang in Llandegla and Llanarmon Churches (but see p.182). A later John Lloyd was Sheriff of Denbighshire in 1551 and his wife Catherine was the daughter of Henry Salusbury who built Llanraeadr Hall in the early 16th Century. Later followed Sir Evan Lloyd, who was also Sheriff of Denbighshire and became a Member of Parliament in 1585. It is believed he fought with the Earl of Leicester and Leicester himself resided at Bodidris from 1563-1578. Leicester was a favourite of Elizabeth lst and used the Hall as a hunting lodge, hence his crest on the front gable of the house. The fable lives on that Elizabeth visited Bodidris to see 'the man she loved but would not marry'.

Another eminent Lloyd was Captain Evan Lloyd, the husband of Mary, daughter of Sir Richard Tannat. He died in 1637and has a beautiful mural tomb in St Garmon's Church, Llanarmon yn Iâl, recording some of his achievements including his family of ten sons and four daughters! The last male heir of the Lloyd family, another Sir Evan, died in 1700 and upon his death Bodidris passed through a female line for three generations. First was Margaret, who was married to Richard Vaughan the third of Cors y Gedol near Harlech. Although she lived some fifty miles away she took a great interest in the life of Llandegla and built many farm houses, including the present Mill Farm House (1736) and The Hand Inn. In 1746 she established an educational charity to help four Llandegla boys to be educated in the English language and place two youths of fourteen years as apprentices each year. She was also responsible for building a school for Llandegla in the churchyard (p.159).

Upon Margaret's death in 1758 aged eighty-three, her son Edward (Evan) Lloyd Vaughan (1709-1791) came to live in Bodidris. He was offered a Parliamentary seat which at first he refused but later accepted. He was an MP from 1774-1791. He died unmarried and, there being no male heir, the estate passed through his sister, Catherine Wynne, wife of Hugh Wynne of Bodysgallen Hall, to their daughter Margaret Mostyn, formerly Wynne, wife of Sir Roger Mostyn Bart (1734-1796). Thus the two estates Cors y Gedol and Bodidris were owned by Margaret Wynne and Sir Roger Mostyn of Mostyn Hall, Flint. Subsequently by maternal descent the estate passed to Sir Thomas Mostyn, Baronet. He also died unmarried and bequeathed Bodidris to his nephew. The Mostyns moved a lot of furniture and contents to Mostyn Hall, but they did leave one suit of armour which stands on the top of the staircase to welcome you to your bedroom.

This was the last of the line of occupation by hereditary means. It is interesting to see the connection by marriage of many large estates which still remain, such as Llanraeadr Hall, Plas yn Iâl, Bodysgallen, Cors y Gedol and Mostyn Hall, Flint.

The Mostyn family were the first to pass on Bodidris by sale in 1843 to Sir Hugh Williams, Baronet of Bodelwyddan, as a shooting lodge. His sister was the Dowager Lady Margaret Willoughby de Broke, who built the Marble Church at Bodelwyddan, consecrated on 23rd August,1860, in memory of her husband Henry Peyto who died in 1852. In 1866 she built a larger church on the present site in Llandegla. Her brother Sir Hugh provided a rent-free rectory (the Old Rectory) and was involved in providing a new village school (the present building) in 1874 and four terraced cottages next door (Church Terrace).

Bodidris was later sold to Ann and Thomas Roberts, whose sixteen children were all born in the house. They were a farming family, raising cattle which were driven down to Suffolk to be sold and geese which were driven to Wrexham, after being 'shod' by being tarred (pp.31,94). In 1919 the estate was sold to Captain Dewhurst of Outringham Park, Cheshire. The Dewhursts have been described as 'the old type of gentry'. They provided work for most of the local inhabitants as farmers, shepherds, game keepers, quarrymen and staff for the house. Bodidris gardeners maintained the churchyard and Mrs Dewhurst provided flowers for the church altar every Sunday. The Dewhurst family also gave the Memorial Hall to the village (pp.54,210).

The Dewhurst family left in 1958 and with them the manorial system. The next owners, the Barritt family, lived in changing times: high

Bodelwyddan October 27th 1868

Dear Sir   I am sorry to hear that
your Neighbour, Mr Jones of Rhos Ddigre,
has got into trouble, thro his Son
and Servant man being caught
Trespassing on your land; Will
you write me particulars of the
case? If it is a serious matter
I will either come up myself or
send Mr Kendall up before the end
of the week to deal with the Matter
but in the meantime, dont allow
any proceedings to be taken against
him. Believe me to be
                    your well wisher
                    Hugh Williams

Mr Hughes
Plas newydd
Llandegla

This letter concerns a little difficulty between two local farms, Plas Newydd and Rhos Ddigre, in 1868. It is signed by Sir Hugh Williams of Bodelwyddan who purchased the Bodidris Estate in 1843. *(Mrs K Beech)*

Bracken cutting on the Bodidris estate in the 1920's. *(Haydn Edwards)*

taxation and maintenance costs caused the breaking up of the large estates. The Barritts broke up the traditional method of small tenant farms and took them over to be managed by estate staff. They sold many of the small farms and other properties, which thus passed into private hands as they remain today. Bodidris was put up for sale again in 1978. It was described thus in the sale particulars:

'one of the finest residential, agricultural and sporting estates in the North West offering a superb Tudor manor house, modern farmsteads, woodlands and land. Well established pheasant and grouse shoot with 3,658 acres of land'.

Sketch of Bodidris *(Carl Hellyn)*

Several parts of the estate and the Hall were bought by Mr David Rattray, a local entrepreneur. He sold the land and some properties to Mr and Mrs Glyn Williams and shortly after repurchased some of the assets. Since then the land and the Hall have been worked independently. The land and moors were bought in 1983 by Mr Brian Draper of Shrewsbury who further broke up the estate in 1986 by selling two moors and Pontystyllod Farm (the Home Farm), the latter being purchased by Mr Tegid Davies, the present owner.

Bodidris Hall has taken on a new role, from a private dwelling to a commercial hotel, firstly run by Mr Robert Best and Mr Peter Smith and since 1994 by an American publisher, Mr William Farden. As Bodidris moves into the millennium taking with it its past let us hope it will continue for many years to come to add to the future pages of history.

9. OUR INSTITUTIONS

Llandegla School

The following has been written by Catherine and Sheila Byrne. Sheila is caretaker and special needs tutor at the school.

There has been a school in Llandegla village since 1745. The original school was the first parochial school in the whole of the Wrexham area. Llandegla Parish shared an educational charity with Llanarmon, founded by Margaret Vaughan of Bodidris and Robert Jones, a brewer from London. In 1746, they gave a tenement or piece of land called Bodlywydd Fechan in trust for the education of eight children from Llanarmon, four from Llandegla, the rest towards an apprentice fund. According to *The History of the Diocese of St Asaph* by D.R.Thomas, a school house was built by subscription in 1777, although a plaque with the names of the trustees on it, which used to be in the school wall, seems to suggest that it was erected in 1791. This plaque is now inset into a garden wall at Accre Hall.

The text as it is on the stone.

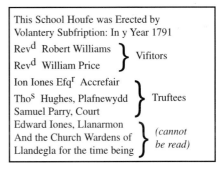

This School Houfe was Erected by Volantery Subfription: In y Year 1791	
Revd Robert Williams Revd William Price	} Vifitors
Ion Iones Efq^r Accrefair Thos Hughes, Plafnewydd Samuel Parry, Court	} Truftees
Edward Iones, Llanarmon And the Church Wardens of Llandegla for the time being	} *(cannot be read)*

The stone from the Llandegla Charity School photographed in the garden of Accre Hall with Mr Owen.
(Janet Handley)

In 1816 the building appears to have been enlarged at the expense of the charity. There is very little trace of this school building left. Opposite Church Terrace there is a relatively large squarish stone built into the churchyard wall which used to be a step to the school. Behind this in the churchyard, there is a gravestone dedicated to the Bloor family. When this grave was first dug an old hearth was found in the bottom of the hole. It is most likely that this belonged to the Charity School.

Information is rather confused regarding the school immediately prior to 1847. It was described in the report of the Commissioners of Inquiry into the State of Education in Wales, 1847, as being held in a loft (possibly either in the Church or in the Hand) "very ill-suited to the purpose, old, very dirty and in bad repair", and the equipment as "in every respect deficient". Apparently, in 1847, Llandegla Charity School transferred from its loft to a new building, built by voluntary subscription with help from Bodidris Hall. It was constructed in the churchyard. This building, according the the report, was damp, floored with stone and the earth of the churchyard rested on one of the main walls to the height of more than four feet above the floor of the school room. The report notes that in 1847, there were about one hundred children in Llandegla of an age to receive instruction, nearly half of whom were unable to pay a penny (1d) a week. The schoolmaster was never trained. Although he spoke English, he spoke it incorrectly but persisted in encouraging the children to speak English even though they were not really capable of doing so.

The clergymen of the two parishes were appointed visitors of each school at the request of the founder of the charity. Appointment of the school master was the responsibility of the trustees of the charity, which resulted in somewhat unsatisfactory people being appointed as masters. By 1847 the rector of Llanarmon, the Reverend Evan Evans, had obtained from the trustees the power of appointing the master and had enrolled the Llanarmon school as a National School but, as the following extract from the Inquiry's report makes clear, the Reverend Williams failed to do the same with regard to Llandegla and it remained a Charity School:

Respecting the master I received the following information from the Rev. E. Williams, incumbent of the parish:

"The clergyman of Llandegla and the clergyman of Llanarmon are appointed visitors of both schools under the will of the founder of the charity. In the case of Llanarmon, the latter clergyman, the Rev Evan Evans, obtained from the Trustees the power of appointing the master, and has had the school enrolled as a National School. I have failed in a similar attempt with regard to the school in Llandegla. I made this attempt in consequence of the improper persons who were appointed as masters. The present master has been discharged as a policeman. In last March (1846) I was informed that the master was found upon the road in a cart in a state of intoxication. In May, I was again informed that the master was seen fighting at the fair. These charges were made to me upon undoubted evidence. I represented the facts to the Trustees. The answer received was, that the Trustees had called the master to account, and had forgiven him. In consequence, I have ceased to act as a visitor, or to take any part of the supervision of the school."

(Signed) E Williams,
Rector of Llandegla

I made enquiries of Mr John Hughes, the acting trustee of the charity who admitted that "complaints had been made, and that he believed the master was too fond of drink; but others were the same, and the man did not make the worse master on that account."

The school finally became Llandegla National School when the present school and school house was opened on January 5th, 1874. The new school was funded by Sir Hugh Williams, Bart., of Bodelwyddan Castle, who had helped to fund the existing school and adjoining cottages when he owned the Bodidris estate in 1866. The architect was almost certainly John Gibson, who had previously designed the church at Llandegla and also the school and the famous estate church at Bodelwyddan. The new school was situated at the bottom of the village hill together with the Hand, formerly the village inn, and St Tecla's Church. It is now a listed building. CADW describes the buildings as a well-designed estate school and school house, which, together with the church, form an attractive group exemplifying the important role played by landed estates as architectural patrons in Wales during the 19th century. This is an extract from a recent CADW report on the school:

"The school and attached school house, now privately owned, is in a quasi-vernacular style forming a T-plan range. It is built with rubble stone and has a slate roof and stone stacks. The gable front has a bellcote with raking offsets and a four centred arched bell opening. Unfortunately the bell has been removed. There is a stone gable coping with kneelers. The upper gable houses a wall clock with a circular moulded stone surround with an inset painted dial. The wall below has a small bell canopy, again with the bell removed. This has a gabled slated roof with arched wooden supports springing from shaped corbels. The west side has two tall three light window openings, a big middle window flanked by narrower windows each side with splayed stone mullions and a boarded door with a rectangular stone lintel. The rear gable has a centrebrick stack flanked by vertical window openings either side.

The school has a pointed arch entry with a studded door. There is a central boarded partition with a wide 24 pane upper window dividing two classrooms. The side walls are boarded to dado level. The east wall has a former fireplace opening, now blocked. A modern ceiling has been inserted at wall plate level, the original room would have been open to the roof, with the arch braced collar trusses springing from stone corbels, which are still visible.

Ysgol Dyffryn Iâl, Llandegla *(Janet Handley)*

In this recent photograph of the school, the windows on the left are those of the School House, where the Headmaster lived until 1969 when it became a private residence. On the right is Church Terrace (p.72). The canopy on the wall was designed to hold a bell, but there has not been one there within living memory. Above is the restored clock, the face is made from traditional slate. Unfortunately the original clock stopped working in the 1960's and the Education Authority refused to pay for the repair. The Chairman of the Governors and owner of Bodidris Estate at that time, Mr R E Barritt, took the clock, had it repaired and had a clock tower built on the stables next to Bodidris Hall (p.151). The clock is still working today and when the wind is blowing in the right direction, it can be heard striking the hours in the village. In 1996, after a failed attempt to get the original clock back, the Community Council installed a replacement. The clock was an important feature in the village with the row of cottages adjoining the school being then known as Time Street, now as Church Terrace.

The arch on the roof was the housing for the bell (the bellcote) operated by the clock that chimed the hours. In the days before people wore watches, the sounding of the hours by the bell would have had an importance which is difficult to visualise today. The bell itself is at Bodidris with the clock. It was this bellrope that was pulled to summon the children to school.

It would be impossible to write a full account of all the events since 1874 until the present time, so instead, through use of school log and minute books and memories of former pupils, here are some of the more significant, interesting and amusing events which have occurred during three periods, the early years between 1874 and 1912 and during the years of the first and second World Wars.

J K Roberts, formerly a student at Saltney Training College, began his duties as first master of the new school on January 5th 1874. The attendance was low, thirty-four pupils in total on account of the cold weather. New desks, maps and books were required. However, within two months the numbers had increased dramatically and there were over a hundred pupils attending the school.

The school was continually closed for reasons usually involving the weather! However attendance also fluctuated due to seasonal commitments; children selling potatoes in May, working in the hay fields in August and harvesting in October, as well as the usual childhood illnesses of measles, ringworm and whooping cough epidemics. Holidays and half holidays were also given for various reasons such as using the schoolroom to erect a platform for a Council meeting on the evening of March 27th 1874. On April 10th 1874, workmen were engaged in erecting the clock high up on the gable end of the school. The clock, made by Joyce of Whitchurch, had a second face on the inside of the school and every Friday, the oldest boy in school would be given the task of winding it. It was also a place where some of the school boys would hide; they would open the doors and actually hide inside the bottom of the clock when they were supposed to be in their lessons but if the teacher found out they were certain to get the cane!

July 27th 1874. Summary of the Inspectors Report on Llandegla National School. (Sunbigh). For Friday June 26th 1874.

"The School which has only been open a few months had made a very good beginning."

"W. Peters Geography."

John Hooson Roberts. (Head Master).
II class. II Division.

William Peters. (Pupil Teacher).

John Owen. Secretary.

A Government inspection took place on an annual basis to make sure the school was complying with the needs of the children.

On the left is a copy of the school's first report, taken from the school's log book, 1874.

However the school was not always as successful in its inspections and the reports varied quite considerably, not many as promising as the first as this summary of the 1885 report reveals. The Reverend John Owen, who signs the report, also visited the school on a weekly basis.

118   1885

Summary of the Report: —
"This school needs attention all round, except in Poetry which was from pretty good to very good — I can recommend no grant for Geography; and the fair merit Grant, and the Grant for the English, and the Grant for needlework I commend with hesitation — The master attempts too much — The mistress should study the code about needlework."

L. W. Jones } 2nd Class Cert.
D. W. Jones }

John Owen. Corresponding Manager

Books were continually required due to the increasing numbers of pupils in the 'standards', and toys for the infants. In 1888 the school numbers in the Juniors were as follows:

Standard	Boys	Girls	Total
1st	12	12	24
2nd	9	3	12
3rd	14	15	29
4th	22	20	42
5th	17	13	30
	74	**63**	**137**

Prizes for good attendance were given. Children attended school until the age of 14 unless they passed their 11+ when they would leave to be educated at Ruthin Grammar School, journeying there by bicycle.

By May 11th 1877 there were one hundred and fifty-one pupils in the school, so that term, Myfanwy Evans and Jane Ellen Harnaman were employed as paid monitors. A group of children were known as "the Charity Boys", and every April they were examined at Llanarmon. A shilling would be given to the Charity boy with the best handwriting and sixpence to the runner-up. On April 26th 1878, the lucky recipients were Thomas Roberts and James Llewelyn.

In October 1889, the flagstone on which the stove was to be placed arrived and by November the first fire was lit in the new stove. It was said to make the school warm and comfortable and that the children worked a lot harder! The children who walked many miles to school from, for example, the Horseshoe Pass would carry a can of milk with them to heat on the stove for morning break.

In 1891, the school curriculum included drawing for the boys and sewing for the girls, this twice a week from 2.20 to 3.00. The girls learned to hem and french seam and made nighties and aprons. Llandegla School had improved considerably and in the same year it had its best ever report following an inspection.

"The Infants and Standard 1 were simply excellent in all subjects and the school as a whole is not far from taking a place amongst the excellent schools in the Diocese."

Below is a copy of a page from an exercise book of a pupil in 1892. The writing is quite impressive, don't you think?

In 1895, the partition to separate the infants from the older children was erected and the school was divided into an infants and a mixed school. In 1897, it was resolved to transfer the school to the St Asaph Diocese Association for the purpose of obtaining grant aid and grants were then given to the school on an annual basis.

In 1907, a meeting was called regarding building a new school but this was rejected. Two years later in response to a suggestion from the head-teacher, the Parish Council attached a metal cup and chain at the Mill for the convenience of the school children. There was a spout with running spring water which was leaded into the wall. To reach this the children had to jump across on stepping stones and a favourite pastime at dinner was to jump the river, ending in many a soaking and perhaps a caning!!

Unfortunately this cup was removed during the war years, as were the railings outside the Memorial Hall.

In 1911, the contract for supplying coal for the school stove was given to Broughton and Plas Power Coal at the rate of twenty shillings and ten pence per ton. A new teacher was appointed at the annual salary of £15. In December 1911 it was noted that a pupil, David Davies, had not missed a single day at school since September 23rd 1904! He was to be presented with a silver watch given by the LEA in such circumstances, costing the princely sum of £2 and made by the watchmaker Mr R M Jones. In July 1912, the school was visited by His Majesty's Inspector Dr Williams and it was decided to congratulate the school staff on their achievements and also to supply them with an enamel jug and two cups for the purpose of drinking water!

Also in 1912, Mrs Dewhurst from Bodidris gave her annual Christmas fayre and tea to the school and in addition pupils received gifts of spinning tops, crackers, oranges, sweets and buns. At Christmas time, there was always a huge tree in the Memorial Hall, lit by candles, under which the presents would be placed. During the summer, pupils were accompanied by staff and occasionally the Rector, to go in procession to Bodidris at the invitation of Mrs Dewhurst who arranged an annual wild flower competition. She presented money prizes for the best bouquets. Mrs Dewhurst commanded great respect throughout the village: the girls had to curtsey to her, the boys to lift their caps and all were scared of her! However, visits to Bodidris always caused great excitement because sometimes the children travelled there sitting on long benches on the back of a lorry belonging to Mr Harrison. The children were also served an afternoon tea of cakes, sandwiches and buns and then they took part in sports. Again there were prizes kept in the summer house, mainly books and spinning tops for the children to choose if they won a race.

During the years of the First World War the little village of Llandegla was rather isolated from reality. In October 1914, it was decided to keep open the teacher's post for a person who had been accepted for active service. The leaflets received from the National War Savings Committee were explained to the pupils and afterwards distributed to their parents. The headmaster, who received a war bonus of £1.38, was instructed to inform and teach the pupils of the privileges and responsibilities attached to the membership of the British Empire! But apart from the framed memorial picture, "Faithful unto Death" being fixed up in the school, life continued as normal for the children, with all seven year olds being presented with a bible by Mrs Dewhurst.

On June 28th, 1919, on hearing that peace had been restored, the head-master rang the school bell and put up a Union Jack in the schoolhouse bedroom window. Early in the morning, the pupils were marched across the road to stand under the sycamore tree (the large tree in front of the Hand), where they sang the Welsh and English National Anthems and gave hearty cheers. A flag was also put up. On October 3rd, in

A postcard published by T P Smith, Pioneer Stores (p.83) between the wars, taken from the former Hand car park. The school and Church Terrace have changed little since. The large tree on the left is the sycamore which is still in front of The Hand. The vigorous larches behind the churchyard are now showing distinct signs of old age! The Cenotaph is rather indistinct on the lower right. This area at the bottom of the village, known locally as the Square, used to be the site of a cattle market. *(Mr Tegla Jones)*

accordance with the wishes of King George V, a holiday of one week was granted to the school to celebrate the peace.

Mrs Gerald Lewis (nee Mabel Parry Roberts) still remembers those days. She was born in 1912, in Tŷ'n y Llidiart, now the home of Ian and Janet Robinson. She was the eldest of five girls, and has lived all her life in or near the village of Llandegla. Her father, Eleazer Parry Roberts, used to live in Hafod Bilston where he farmed and her mother Eva Roberts came from Cae Gwydd, Treuddyn, then Fron Botes, known as "Happy Valley", beyond Bodidris.

All her education was in the school at Llandegla where all the lessons were in English despite the fact that Welsh was the first language for most children. Mabel remembers the hard winters when she had to walk to school and on one occasion she, together with several other children, were very late because they were playing in the snow on their way. The game was to lie down in the snow and make impressions with the arms and legs stuck out at an angle, followed by some of the children testing the image to see if they could fit into the template in the snow. There was a gang of children who were late and the Headmaster lined them all up and caned them on their hands: the first and only time for Mabel! Children who lived a long way from school used to take their own dinners and they were kept warm on a large black coal boiler. There were often mishaps such as a tin blowing up and shedding its contents over the pupils and the classroom!

At the outbreak of the Second World War, a school managers' meeting was held on September 8th, 1939 to make arrangements to accommodate the evacuees. They were to be taught in the Memorial Hall. In January 1940 the Government evacuees arrived from Liverpool but through some misunderstanding, they were unable to use the Hall and the Headmaster made arrangements for them to be taught with the village children. The Director of Education met Captain Dewhurst from Bodidris and the Headmaster of Lister Drive School, Liverpool, at the Memorial Hall and it was decided at the meeting that the Hall would be open to the evacuees the next day.

Life continued normally enough for the children despite the war but there was a mumps epidemic at the end of January, and because of this and the severe weather conditions, not a child made an appearance at the school between January 30th and February 5th when four children attended but the school medical officer advised closure of the school until February 7th so the four children went home! Because the epidemic spread further, only six children attended on February 7th so the Headmaster was advised to close the school until February 19th.

St David's Day, March 1st 1940, saw the evacuees joining the local children in Llandegla school to sing Welsh airs together. In July of the same year, there was a mixed concert held in the Memorial Hall where the village pupils acted a play "The White Garland", and evacuees gave an exhibition of folk dancing. Even though there were fights between some of the village boys and the evacuees, most mixed quite happily. Children of Llandegla and children from Liverpool went to Sunday school and were confirmed together and many of the evacuees still come from Liverpool to visit friends in Llandegla today.

However 1940 was not just a year of singing, dancing and acting. On September 9th 1940 attendance was again low at Llandegla School because of the air-raids the previous week. Bombs had been dropped very close to Cae Madoc farm, Hafod yr Abad farm and Pentre Isaf and the children of Ddôl Ddu, where a bomb had fallen dangerously close to the farm and killed a horse, were not present at school during the following week (p.65). During the August holidays in 1941, workmen were engaged in fixing props to the ceiling in the girls' cloakroom as protection from possible air-raids. On October 20th there was an air raid and the following morning the headmaster was informed by the local constable that there was an unexploded land mine in the Mill field, about 300 yards from the school. The children were sent home.

On VE day, May 8th 1945, Germany surrendered unconditionally to the allied nations and there was a two-day holiday to celebrate the peace. After the Prime Minister's broadcast announcing the end of the war, there was a short service of thanksgiving for the termination of the hostilities and Llandegla School bell was rung after a silence of many years.

The school celebrates the coronation of Queen Elizabeth II in 1953. The Coronation Queen is Cynthia Beech (Mill Farm). Also pictured are:
(Left to Right) Mr Rathbone who crowned the Queen; Councillor Mr W.R. Jones (Belle View); Miss O.H.Roberts who made the dress; and Mr Herbert, Headteacher.
(Mr Tegla Jones)

In 1980 Llandegla school became an *Ysgol Efeilliol*: it was twinned with Bryneglwys school to prevent the closure of these small rural schools because of low numbers, a far cry from the late 1890's. In 1989, the joint school was renamed Ysgol Dyffryn Iâl meaning the school of the valley of Yale, unifying both schools under one name although they are in fact five miles apart. The two village schools are still joined under one Governing Body and one Head. The two sites as far as possible operate as a single school which allows work, equipment and evaluation procedures to be shared. The curriculum is strengthened through this and the children have a larger peer group to mix with. However externally little has altered and if you listen on a calm summer's evening, you may hear the sound of children's voices. Past or present: who's to know?!

The school photograph is an annual event. Here is a small selection from the hundred or so photographs that have been taken.

In the school yard, 1901 *(Mrs Gwen Hughes)*

The youngest of the three classes of 1914. The teacher is Miss Jones *(Mr Tegla Jones)*

172

1914: Class 1, also in the schoolyard. Mr Robert Williams, Headmaster, is on the left.

Top row: Sue Williams (Gate House); Winnie Jones (Tafarn y Gâth); Harry Evans (Cae Madog); William Watkin (Hen Giât)

Middle row: Olwen Evans (Cae Madog); ? Coles (Plas Yn Iâl); Mary Davies (Minfford & The Hand); Bob ? (Bryn Awel); Tommy Williams (Giât y Nant); John Owen Jones (*Jack the Sailor)* (the village); Stanley Jones (Pant y Ffordd & Efail Rhos); Leonard Davies (Tegla Cottage)

Bottom row: Lizzie ?(Garden Cottage, Hen Giât); Edith Jones (3 Church Terrace); Olive Jones (Ffynnon Wen); Catherine Elizabeth ? (Pen Stryt Farm); Marion Jones (*m. Ted Edwards)* (Bodawen); Mary Jones *(Tegla Jones' mother)* (Rhewl Glyn Rhys); Dan Jones (3 Church Terrace)

1914: the older children. **Back row from left to right**: William J McLellan (Brenhinlle Fawr); Idris Jones (Fynnon Wen); Alun Jones *(Ehedydd Iâl's grandson)* (Tafarn y Gâth); Emlyn Jones (Tan y Graig); Harry Coles (Plas yn Iâl); ? another member of the Coles family. Doris Jones (Fynnon Wen) is sitting second left; Ben Jones (Pen y Stryt), first on the right. *(Both from Mr Tegla Jones)*

173

1923: "Rose Day" at the school. Flora Edwards aged 5 is in the front row, fifth from the left. *(Mrs Flora Edwards)*

1950: Mr T R Herbert, Headmaster, is holding Tuffy, his dog. Miss O. Roberts of Green Park is the teacher, on the left. *(Mrs Sylvia Jones, nee Beech)*

Back row from the left: Alun Edwards (Fron Haul); Arnold Bellis (Ffynnon Wen); Cynthia Beech *(Coronation Queen, 1953, p.171)* (Erw Fawr); Rose Francis (Rhos Ddigre); Merion Williams (Bodawen); Joan Carr (Church Terrace); Doreen Nixon (Pontystyllod); Una Wotton (Old Gate); David Morris (the village); John Jones (Tŷ Ucha); Clive Hindley (Council Houses).

Second row: Margaret Beech (Erw Fawr); Glenys Beech, (Erw Fawr); Maureen Powell (Tan y Fron); Jeff Lewis (Council Houses); Gareth Oldfield (Pennant Cottage); John Evans (Pen Dinas); Gordon Milton (Caemadog Isa); Brian Kendall (Plas yn Coed); Gareth Williams (Ddôl Ddu); Josephine Jones (Gloppa); Gwendoline Grace (Hand Inn); Elizabeth Jones (Bodidris Cottages).

Third row: David Kendall (Plas yn Coed); Muriel Milton (Caemadog Isa); Ann Lewis (Council Houses); Amy Roberts (Tŷ'n y Llidiart); Diane Rennie (Plough Inn); Delia Rennie (Plough Inn); Betty Carr (Church Terrace); Dorothy Jones (Gloppa); Susan Parry (Arfryn Cottage); Pat Howard (?); Danny Edge (Chweleiriog Goch).

Front Row: Derek Owen (Council Houses); Joe Edge (Chweleiriog Goch); Allan Lewis (Council Houses); Willie Jones (Council Houses); David Jones (Isfryn); Colin Hindley (Council Houses); Neil Carr (Church Terrace).

175

c. 1955: some of the juniors in the cloakroom. There were so many in the school at that time that the cloakroom had to be used as a classroom. *(Mrs Flora Edwards)*

Top row from the left: Kenny Bloor (No 2 Village Cottages); Hazel Edwards (No 1 Village Cottages); Gwilym Jones, (*the Minister's son*) (Llys Myfyr)

Front row: Elfed Jones (London House); Neil Carr (Church Terrace); Gwendolyn Bellis (Ffynnon Wen); Mark Lloyd (Hafan).

1960: also taken in the cloakroom. *(Mrs Flora Edwards)*

Back row: Haydn Edwards (No 1 Village Cottages); David Davies (No 2 Village Cottages); Prysor Williams (Pennant Isa); Graham Falshaw (*the Bailiff's son*) (Pontystyllod); Gareth Morris Davies *(Boris)*; Ifor Jones (Gorphwysfa: now The Old Rectory).

Middle Row: Elwyn and Glyn Edwards (Fron Haul Farm); Gaynor Robson (Maes Maelor); Bethan Beech (Mill Farm); Megan Smith (Tŷ'n y Llydiart); Goronwy Jones (*the Minister's son*) (Llys Myfyr); ? (Tŷ Hir).

Front row: Emyr Owen (Bodawen Farm); Gwenda Jones (?Rose Cottage); David Barritt (Bodidris Hall); Anona Davies (No 2 Village Cottages); Gwynfor Smith (Tŷ'n y Llydiart).

Seated on the floor: Delwyn Edwards (Pen y Stryt Cottages); Arwel Jones (*the Minister's son*) (Llys Myfyr).

1969: in the school playground. *(Mr and Mrs K Bellis)*

Back row: ?; ?; Mrs Pugh (teacher); David Pluke; Trevor Davies; Gwyn Lightfoot; John Forster; Robin Dyke; Medwyn Owen; Mark Astles

Second row: Richard Lloyd; Elwyn Owen; Spencer Belton; Roger Faulkner; ?; Llywelyn Owen; Julian Astles (?); Stephen Hughes.

Third row: David Prydderch; Mark Prydderch (?); ?; ?; Anne Jones; June Davies; Jayne Astles; David Jones.

Front row: Stephen Forster; Helen Price; Julia Hughes; ?; ?; Gwenan Edwards; Gaynor Price; Tirwen Roberts; Karen Bellis.

1970: the infant class. *(Mr and Mrs K. Bellis)*

Back row: Ann Wyn Jones; Melanie Owen; David Prydderch.

Middle row: Karen Bellis; Jayne Clark; Gaynor Price; Stephen Forster.

Front row: John Morris; Julie Hughes; Sandra Bellis; Dawn Evans; Martin Edwards.

177

1974: *(Mr Tegla Jones)*

1988:
*(Mrs Sheila
Byrne)*

Back row: Melanie Ashley; Jenny Lawton; Clare Mooney; Thomas Trow; Ieuan White; Kelly Dyke; Catherine Byrne

Middle row: Mark Pluke; John Lloyd; Llion Faulkner; Patricia Hilton; Marie Lloyd; Dawn Harrison; Natalie Mooney; Molly Irvine; Amanda Swindells; Menna Lloyd

Sitting in front: Robert Dyke; Liam Byrne; Paul Harrison

Teachers: Mr Emyr Jones (left); Mrs Nesta Evans (right)

1992: the Memorial Hall was used to accommodate
all the children   *(Mrs Sheila Byrne)*

Back row: Johnathan Clegg; Mark Carrigan; Liam Byrne; Chris Park; Marie Lloyd; Nia Pinchbeck; Matthew Bellis; Liam Roberts; Jamie Carrigan; Rhys Hughes

Second row: Robert Dyke; Melissa Mooney; Patricia Hilton; Wyn Davies; Lloyd Davies; Dawn Harrison; Vicky Anyon; David Davies; Menna Lloyd; Paul Harrison; Elizabeth Pinchbeck; Ian Jones

Third row: Amanda Swindells; Matthew George; Daniel Meecham; Alun Ellis; Peter Harrison; Mark Pluke; John Lloyd; Natalie Mooney; Gwyn Ellis; Samantha Matischok; Sion Hughes; Meirion Davies

Fourth row: Kara McGahy; Bethan Jones; Kayleigh Curtis; Katy Davies; Eira Davies; Sally Carrigan; Donna Howells; Stacy Davies; Ellen Edwards; Nina Davies; Catherine Price; Bethan Davies; Leanne Davies

Front row: Joe Mault; Iestyn Tango; Simon Davies; James Matischok; Dafydd Hughes; Andrew Boland; Aled Harrison; James Clegg; Ian Evans; Chris Moore; Tim Moore; Thomas Mooney

Teachers: Left: Roger Haywood (Head); Carol Mault (Nursery Nurse); Nesta Evans. Right: Gwen Ellis; Sioned Edwards; Ann McKee

The Millennium School Photograph in front of
the stage curtain in the Memorial Hall
(Mrs Sheila Byrne)

Front row: Robin Myers; Courtney Law; Ellen Wonderly; Robert Thompson; Daniel Philipson; Rhys Jackson; Sara Mault; Rachel Law.
Second Row: Thomas Clarke; Rose Hiles; Jack Anyon; Daniel Swygart; Dominic Chamberlain; Michael Abraham; Jessica Law; Katie Rosen; Jevon Bhalla; Polly Williams Blythen; Tom Walker; Melissa Bartlett; Zoe Pritchard; Awen Mon Roberts.
Third Row: Francis Matthews; Lydia David; Kyza Edwards; Steven Hampson; Ben Davies; Arwyn Davies; Sian Evans; Jamie Conway; Hannah Jones; Siwan Jones; Sam Mault; Billy Evans.
Fourth Row: Natasha Clarke; Sophie Bhalla; Joshua Davey; Benjamin Davies; Sioned Davies; Ben David; Helen Dobbing; Jessica Nunn; Joshua Davies; Iorwerth Jones; Siobhan Gledhill; Christopher Campbell.
Back Row: John Evans; Gabriel Banks; Dion Hughes; Emily Nunn; Emily Rosen; Amber Clemence; Charlotte Higson Ffoulkes; Christopher Jones; Elliot Banks; Daniel Bhalla; Jasmine Rosen.

Teachers: Left: Nicola Williams (Llandegla, Infants); Nia Hughes (Nursery Assistant); Ruth Jones (Bryneglwys, Infants).
Right: Eryl Roberts (Headteacher); Rhian Davies (Ancillary Support Worker); Mair Edwards (Deputy Head).

St Tecla's Church

The Church in Llandegla is dedicated to St Tecla (correctly it should be 'Thecla', it is 'Tegla' in Welsh). When she was in her teens she heard St Paul preach on his missionary journey through Turkey in about 50 AD. Despite family opposition, she became a Christian. She came from Iconium which is the modern Konya in Turkey, about three hundred miles southeast of Istanbul. After miraculously surviving a pyre and being thrown to the beasts, she spent the rest of her life ministering to the sick, helping the poor and spreading the word of God. Her life was spent partly in travel and partly in monastic life in her cave. She died when she was nearly ninety, the first Christian virgin martyr. There are two conflicting legends about how she died. One says that she was martyred by Nero. The other says that she was set upon by men of 'evil intent'. She fled to a nearby rock which opened to engulf her, so escaping her attackers. There is an Orthodox Christian church on this site in Mullulia in Syria dedicated to St Tecla which is still a shrine for pilgrimage for the sick. This may explain her connection with Llandegla where the Well had a tradition of curing those who suffered from epilepsy (p.16). The dedication may have come from the returning crusaders, but the healing powers and ritual associated with St Tecla's Well are pre-Christian. The only other active church in Wales with the same dedication is the Norman Church of Llandegley, near Llandrindod Wells. There is a ruined church dedicated to St Tecla on the little island beneath the old Severn Bridge. Among her many attributes she was the patron saint of people who travel on ferries, so the location of this church is entirely appropriate. There is a relic of St Tecla in the Kikkos Monastery in the Troodos Mountains in Cyprus. St Paul is known to have visited Cyprus, so this may be the connection.

Our church is relatively modern, being built in 1866 as a replacement for an earlier building. The architect was John Gibson, who also designed the much more elaborate marble church at Bodelwyddan.

The chandelier is Flemish, being made around 1450-1500 AD. It is reputed to have come from Valle Crucis Abbey, but it is more probable

The chandelier with the east window behind.
(*Len Wilkinson*)

that it was brought over by Sir Evan Lloyd, a member of the Lloyd family of Bodidris, who fought in the Low Countries under Leicester. Its symbolism of the figure of the Virgin Mary in prayer surrounded by light from the candles would have been appreciated as well as the craftsmanship. (Tegla Davies in his autobiography tells of how when he was at school in the village people thought the central statue was that of Queen Victoria!).

Behind the chandelier is the East Window, which used to be in St Asaph Cathedral. The restoration of the cathedral and the rebuilding of the church coincided which enabled the window to be transferred to Llandegla. It is a rare example of a smoked glass made in Birmingham in 1779 by Frances Eginton. The central figure of Jesus is surrounded by cherubs enacting his future crucifixion. The stained glass window in the nave is a memorial to Glyn Price Jones and Francis Campbell Jones (pp.68-70). The font is considerably older than the church.

Llandegla celebrated the centenary of its church in grand style over a weekend in 1966. There were three main events: an exhibition, entertainment in the Memorial Hall and a service in the church itself.

The entertainment on the Saturday evening included performances by the children of the village, pop music for the teenagers, plays, singing and more. The Memorial Hall was so packed there was standing room only: a memorable evening for everyone. On the following day a full church celebrated evensong. Members of Bethania and Pisgah chapels attended, together with a coachload of people from Bryneglwys. The bilingual service was taken by the Reverend T. Ivor Williams, the rector, with the Welsh lesson being read by the Rev. Giraldus Morris, former minister of Penstryt chapel.

The aim of the exhibition was to assemble a collection of everyday household items and memorabilia from just one hundred years, but in the event there was a fascinating collection of articles from many years back. There were expensive clothes, old bibles and prayer books, prints and paintings, legal documents, letters, everyday household utensils and much more. The exhibition was a revealing insight into life as it was in 'grandad's day'.

One exhibit in particular recalled a family tradition of service to the church. A copper warming pan had been used by Daniel Jones, sexton of St Tecla's Church from 1861-1902. He was succeeded by his son, Thomas, and then his grandson, Daniel. It was perhaps a potent reminder of the stability of the village, over a hundred years of service by only three generations of one family.

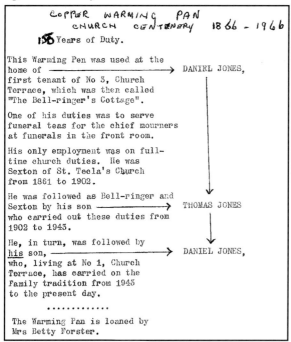

Exhibit label from the exhibition. *(Mrs Betty Foster)*

183

Ultimately this service was to last for a hundred and forty years: the last Daniel Jones, 'Uncle Dan', died in 2000. The following appreciation by Mr William Owen, translated from the Welsh by Phil Clark, appeared in *Y Llan* in October 2000 (for Welsh version see p.242):

"Our dear friend Daniel Jones, Sexton for the Parish for sixty years, who followed his father and grandfather in this venerable office, has died. For him this was not just a job but a vocation. He was behind seven rectors in his time, and they all had a good word for him and valued his ready help on every occasion.

It was a pleasure to see the church full of people of every denomination at a service to give thanks for Daniel Jones' life of service. The service was taken by the Reverend Brian Hall and the lesson (The Wisdom of Solomon 3: 1-9) was read by William Owen, Warden to the rector.

A few years ago, in the company of Huw Jones, the Auxilliary Bishop at that time, we had the opportunity to give thanks to the

genial sexton for fifty years of untiring service to the church of God. On that occasion Beryl Lightfoot sang a number of penillion to salute this affable man and loyal friend, a ready benefactor, his smile while smoking his pipe and his enjoyment of the traditions and old customs of the Church."

Dan Jones outside the school playground in the summer of 1963. The rough grass on the right has gone, replaced by the village car park and a neatly clipped hedge.
(Mrs Maisie Evans)

There is a plaque to the memory of Dan Jones on the West Wall (on the left as you enter the Church), where he had his seat. It is by the bellrope: one of his duties was to ring the bell for church services. Further along the same wall is a list of the forty-one rectors who have served the parish of Llandegla from 1529 to the present day. The last name is the Reverend Brian Hall who will retire in January 2002. Another multi-denominational service will mark this occasion.

The occasion will also celebrate the tradition of long service upheld by the organist, Mrs Dorothy Williams, who succeeded Mrs Smith of Tŷ'n y Llidiart as organist. In 2002 she will have completed fifty years in her post.

The chapels *(Mr Tegla Jones)*

There were five chapels in Llandegla, but only two, Bethania Chapel and Pisgah Chapel, are now in regular use.

The starting date of the Methodist cause in Llandegla, leading to the establishment of the **Bethania Calvanistic Methodist Chapel**, is uncertain. It is said that Rev J Eleias and Rev W Roberts of Amlwch preached in the hay yard belonging to Dafydd Parry y Llan in 1816 and that services were held in an old house near to the mill. Then in 1819 the cause moved to the Old Gate House on Old Gate Lane. It is reported that

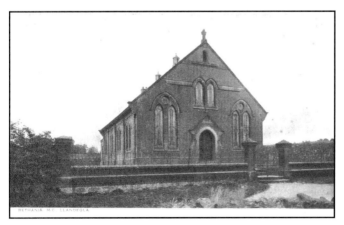

A pre-war photo-graph of Bethania Chapel.
(Mr. Tegla Jones)

185

there was a very successful Sunday School there. The cause remained in the Gate House for eight years until it was decided that a larger building was required. Building was started in the present position in 1827 and opened for services in 1828. In 1840 we are told that a Mr Roberts came to live in Bodidris (p.154). He was a great help to the cause. His large family and servants swelled the congregation.

It was decided to refurbish the chapel in 1844. In the wake of the revival of 1859 the chapel was extended in 1861 at a cost of £300. It was again rebuilt in 1903 and this is the building which stands today.

The Congregationalists' cause began in Llandegla around 1800, meeting in the house of one Thomas Parry. Students from the academy at Wrexham and Mr Benjamin Evans of Ruthin would preach there regularly and a Sunday School was also held. Sometime before 1813 the barn at Pen y Stryd Farm was adapted for worship.

The first chapel was built in the present position in October 1817 for £200 and was looked after by Mr John Griffiths of Trelech until 1839 when there was a revival. In 1840 the old chapel and house were demolished and a new larger chapel was built. This chapel was called **Pisgah.** In 1843 Mr Samuel Evans of Rhos was chosen as minister, and remained for forty years. During the first twenty years of his ministry he would walk every Sunday from Rhosllanerchrugog (near Wrexham) to

A pre-war photograph of Pisgah Chapel. Later a gate was put into the wall to give access from Old Gate Lane.

(Mr. Tegla Jones)

Reverend Samuel Evans (left, seated) of Pisgah Chapel with his wife, daughters, son-in-law and grandchildren Nesta and David Hughes, in the early 1900s outside their home, Brynhyfryd.
(Mr. Jim Hughes)

Llandegla. In those days this was the only means of transport for ordinary folk, but even so it was a considerable commitment. Later he lived at Brynhyfryd, which was built in 1861 (p.38).

Within six years the chapel had a new minister, Mr Ben Davies. He stayed for three years until he moved to Pant Teg, becoming well known throughout Wales as a hymnwriter. In 1898 he was succeeded by Mr

Celebrating the 200th anniversary of the Sunday School in Wales in Pisgah Chapel in 1985
(Mr. Tegla Jones)

Tonlas Hughes who stayed until 1911. During his ministry the chapel was re-designed as it is today at a cost of £630.

During the twentieth century there have been five ministers, the last being Rev Bromley Rees, now residing in Coedpoeth.

Another Methodist Sunday School was held in the corn loft at Pentre Isaf Farm from 1844 until 1848. It then moved to join the Sunday School that was held at the Old Gate (Yr Hen Giât, previously a toll house, pp.36,38). This was rather far for people from Tai Newyddion and nearby to travel, so they returned and held the Sunday School at The Traveller's Rest (p.101). In 1854 permission was given to build a chapel, called **Salem Pentre Bwlch Calvanist Methodist Chapel**, opposite Pentre Bwlch farm. Originally it was just a schoolroom without seating. In 1874 because of an increase in the congregation seating was brought in. In 1878 a chapel house was built.

The chapel was rebuilt and enlarged in 1910. The foundation stone from the rebuilding reads:

SALEM PENTRE BWLCH

ADDOLDY

Y METHUDISTIAID CLAFINAIDD

A ADEILADWYD YN Y FLWYDDYN 1854

AILADEILADWD A HELAETHWYD

YN Y FLWYDDYN 1910

"CEDWCH FY SABOTHAU A PHERCHWCH

FY NGHYSSEGR, YR ARGLWYDD

YDWYF FI"

A literal translation:
Salem Pentre Bwlch
The Methodist Calvanistic
place of Worship
Built in the year 1854
Rebuilt and enlarged in the year 1910
"Keep my Sabbath and respect
my Sanctuary, The Lord
I am"
(Mrs Dilys Davies)

Dilys Davies (p.51) was caretaker from 1947-52. She cleaned the chapel and gave the minister tea every other Sunday. She lived in the chapel house with Efan and her family. There was no water or electricity: water for washing and heating the chapel had to be carried from The Traveller's Rest. Drinking water came from a well at Pentre Bwlch Farm. In the winter of 1947 Dilys's family had to walk all the way to Llangollen for bread.

The Salem Pentre Bwlch Chapel and Chapel House were demolished in 1967. The rubble from this and the Traveller's Rest was used as foundations for a cattle shed at Pentre Isaf.

A christening party outside Salem Pentre Bwlch Chapel which took place in 1953. **Left to right:** Mrs Hughes; Mrs Davies (Cae Mawr); Elsa Davies; Mrs Eileen Davies holding baby Gareth; Mr Jones; Mr Jones, Minister; Miss Jones; Mr L Jones, behind Mrs Jones; Mr Davies; Mr Harry Jones. *(Mrs Eileen Davies)*

The history of the **Beth-Hogla/Seion Chapel** goes back to 1801 when Mr Jones, Bathafarn and John Jones, Chweleiriog, started the Wesleyan Cause locally. When living in London they had been influenced by Wesley and Whitfield. They rented a loft at the Cross Keys for £1 10s which was considered to be too much as access was through the living quarters. By 1812 there were twenty-eight members and J Jones Esq. of Accre (son of Mr Jones, Chweleiriog) provided.a plot of land on which to build a chapel. This was behind the Blue Bell (now the Village Shop). It is now a workshop. The ground rent (lease) was eight shillings annually and it cost £126 to build. Thirty years later, after being in financial trouble, Lord Mostyn gave the Wesleyans a plot for a new chapel which opened on June 13th and 14th of 1842 with one hundred and fifty-eight seats. It was finally closed in 1914 due to a dwindling congregation. It was bought by Mrs Dewhurst of Bodidris and left to the parish to be used as the Memorial Hall (pp.54, 209).

Both Ehedydd Iâl (p.43) and Tegla Davies worshipped at this chapel. Edward Tegla Davies was a well known and greatly respected Wesleyan minister and a popular author. He was born at Bryn Tirion on May 31st 1880, the son of William and Mary Davies. His father was a quarryman who worked at Moel y Faen (on the Horseshoe Pass). The family moved to Llyn Rhys and then to Foel Gwrachen (now Glascoed). He had two sisters, Mary Ellen and Hannah and two brothers, Rhys Alyn and Lemuel. He had three children, Dyddgu, Arfor and Gwen.

Parch. E. Tegla Davies *(Mr Tegla Jones)*

He became a minister in 1904, leading a very active professional life until he retired in 1946. He first preached in Coedpoeth, and then ministered in Abergele, Felinheli, Tregarth, Llanrhaeadr yn Mochnant (where he spent the years of the First World War), Denbigh, Manchester, Liverpool and Bangor. He presided over the Methodist Assembly in 1937 and was on a joint committee of the Calvanistic Methodists and the Wesleyans in 1927, drawing up the resulting book. After retirement he was honoured with a doctorate by the University of Wales.

He was a prolific writer, publishing around thirty five books of all sorts. In addition to his novels and religious books, he was editor of three periodicals: *Y Winllan* (The Vineyard) from 1920-28, *Yr Efrydydd* (The Student) from 1931-35 and *Cyfres Pobun* from 1944-50. His children's books were influential as well as giving great pleasure: in 1925 he wrote the first book in Welsh about space for children. He enchanted generations of children, he added to our few important novels in the Welsh language and he gave strength and message to the essay form of writing. Islwyn Ffowc Elis said of him that he was "a great writer, a great Christian and a great man". Prof W J Gruffydd states in the Encyclopaedia Brittanica, "The work of Tegla Davies bears many traits of pure genius".

During his life he never forgot his roots, returning to Llandegla every summer for a holiday. He died on October 9th 1967 and was buried in Tregarth.

The two cottages that made up Bryn Tirion in Old Gate Lane in 1970, probably much as they were when Tegla Davies was born there in the lefthand cottage. They were built in the late 1700s. They have since been made into one and extended. The gable end in the background is Brynhyfryd (p.38) *(Reproducted with permission from Denbighshire Record Office, Ruthin)*

The building which was the **Moriah Chapel** stands on the left by the junction of the B5431 to Llanarmon and the old road to Ruthin via Graigfechan. A Sunday school had started to meet in Tŷ Newydd, the farm opposite. In 1895 Moriah Chapel was built and the Sunday school continued there. It is labelled as 'Sunday School' on the 1912 OS Map. The photograph below shows a group outside Moriah Chapel in 1977, on the occasion of the presentation of the Thomas G. Medal to Mr John Beech (Perthichwarae) for his faithful attendance at the Sunday school. The chapel closed in 1993 and is now a workshop.

Left to right: Llywelyn Owen; Ieuan Williams; Jean Evans; Hilary Morris; Prysor Williams; Mrs B Owen; Stuart Morris; Mrs M Williams; Mr R H Edwards; Mr J T Hughes; Mrs J T Hughes; Mrs L M Beech; Mr J Beech (wearing the medal); Mrs M E Edwards; Mrs W R Jones; Mr I Williams; Mrs M Edwards; Mr T Beech; Arwyn Roberts; Meinir Roberts; Mrs H Roberts; Helen Price; Matthew Price; Margaret Jones; Gaynor Price; Elfor Morris; Eurgain Edwards; Mrs E Morris; The Rev. Philip de la Haye. *(Denbighshire Free Press)*

A recent view of Moriah Chapel. The farm buildings behind are part of Castell Farm. *(Alan Scrivner)*

Moriah Chapel in 1985, decorated with flowers for the celebrations for the centenary of the foundation of the Sunday School Movement in Wales *(Llywelyn Owen)*

10. OUR SOCIAL SOCIETIES AND ACTIVITIES: PAST AND PRESENT

It reflects well on the village that there are so many active groups, those below as well as other activities that take place in the Memorial Hall and elsewhere. Each of the current societies has been described by a society member for the Millennium book.

Friendly societies

Friendly Societies flourished before the days of National Insurance and the National Health Service. They were established to help their members in times of sickness, accident, old age and to help widows. Money was paid out for members' funerals and that of the first wife only.

The **Union Friendly Society** was one of three societies who met in Dafarn Dywyrch, The Crown, The Hand and the Blue Bell (pp.90-101). A meeting was held on the last Saturday of each month where each member had to pay a shilling to the treasurer. New members had to pay an entrance fee of three shillings. The funds were kept in a box with three locks and three keys. Members could not gain any benefit unless they had been a member for two years and there was at least £250 in the fund. In 1834 the leading members of the society were Thomas Jones (Rhos), Richard Roberts (Bryniau), James Owens (Dafarn Dywyrch) and Thomas Davies who was secretary and treasurer.

The rules for members, published in 1834, were strict. A prospective member had to be balloted by existing members and would not have been acceptable unless he was "a person of good and fair character of a sober and peaceable disposition, and is at that time free from any infirmities of body or above the age of thirty". Discipline was maintained by the imposition of fines for a variety of offences: refusing to join the committee, be a steward or visit a sick member within twenty-four hours cost six pence. Members who cursed and swore or were drunk had to pay a shilling. If any member feigned sickness, committed a crime or failed to pay monthly contributions or fines he was expelled. Despite these draconian measures, the rules state "that the concerns of this Society be conducted in a friendly and charitable Manner".

A dinner was held annually on Whit Monday. Each member had to be in church by 11.00 am. If absent he would have to give a contribution towards the cost of the dinner: "any member who shall cause any dispute or disturbance on that day or shall carry or dispose of liquor to any person not belonging to the society, he shall for every offence forfeit two shillings".

Tegla Davies describes his memories of the day:

> *The most important day in the year for the societies was the day of the annual dinner and march. The members and onlookers, adults and children, would line the street by the Methodist Chapel. The band would be ready resplendent in their red coats, navy blue trousers with a red stripe, caps had a chin strap. The Clerk, Robert Jones the Mill, would take a roll call, the members then forming in pairs to march behind the band. They marched up the hill to Penystryd and on to the Plough, proceeding to the Crown a drink would be ready for the band in both places. The children would hold the Bandsmen's cards for them to play in front of both inns. Everyone then made their way to church.*

> *After the service on to the dinner held in the stable loft of the Hand. The menu remained the same every year. Lamb, split peas, potatoes and mint sauce, followed by Christmas pudding. After dinner the games would start, donkey races, three legged races, climbing the soapy pole (a live piglet was placed on the top as the winner's prize).*

As implied above, the membership of the Union Friendly Society was for men only, but there was a parallel society for the ladies, the **Llandegla Female Friendly Society**, founded in 1840. Thomas Davies was also secretary at that time. It later became the Female Benefit and Assurance Society. It seems that the monthly meetings, where the members made their payments, were social occasions as well. Each member brought

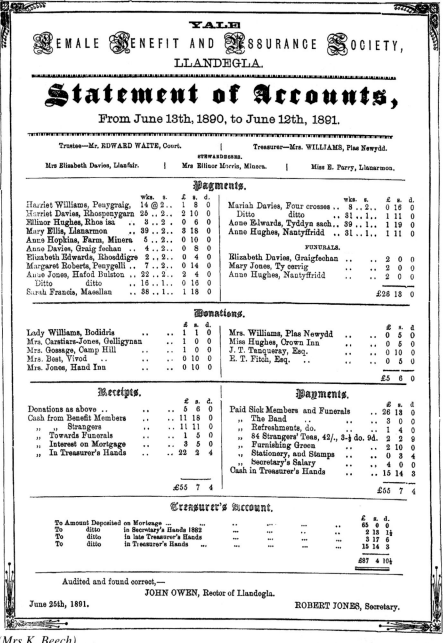

(Mrs K. Beech)

their own teacup to each meeting. These cups were supplied by the society: rather shallow cups without a handle. The rules and methods of handling money were similar to those for the men. Membership was for females between the ages of eighteen and forty-five. No one of ill health, ill reputation or of a weak constitution was to be admitted to the society. The misdemeanours for which a member could be expelled were also similar, with this addition "...if she be found unlawfully pregnant (whether she married or not before the birth of the child)". It seems that some in most need would have been excluded.

The ladies would also march and have a service in Llandegla Church, after which they would proceed to the Blue Bell for their dinner. They had their own band (which was still functioning in 1891 according to the accounts shown here) for these occasions. After dinner came the dancing. Pine branches (possibly cut from those by the Blue Bell, p.90) were placed either side of the path leading to the field where the dancing took place. The ladies, resplendent in their ribbons, would march to the music provided by the band. The Mistress of Ceremonies was a lady from a nearby village known locally as *Ann 'Rhen Draed* (Ann of the old feet) because of their dexterity whilst dancing. Everyone would follow her lead.

The Llandegla Female Friendly Society ('Clwb Merched') *(Mr Tegla Jones)*

The Llandegla Women's Institute *(Janet Handley)*

The Llandegla Women's Institute was formed on April 27th 1949. The formation of Llandegla, together with Bylchau, Tan y Fron, Marchweil and Rhosnesni, all of which were established in 1947, made the total of seventy-two Institutes in the Denbighshire Federation. In 1980, the Federation had eighty-eight affiliated Institutes. The trend now is a falling membership, and there are only seventy-six Institutes in the Federation. The number of members has fluctuated from the highest in 1950 of fifty-one members, to an average of twenty-three in 1980, to our current membership of thirty-one. This increase has been due to the closure of Bryneglwys in 1991 followed by Llanarmon yn Iâl in 1996 when some of their members joined us. We have not changed our name but membership covers Llandegla and "district" geographically.

The first meeting was held on May 16th 1949. At this time men were returning from the Second World War, food was still rationed but restricted clothes allocation had ended. The first task the W.I. undertook was to apply for food permits. In the early years, becoming a member was not just taken for granted: all new members had to have their "application to join" considered by "the committee". This is not the case today. When a member married the Institute gave her a present such as fish eaters, fish knives and forks or fruit spoons. If a member gave birth to a child the Institute gave her a cheque for ten shillings and sixpence. Regretfully no-one has qualified for such a gift for a very long time!

The founder members must have been very good organisers because a typical meeting included several aspects: the singing of Jerusalem; apologies; business (a) local (b) county (c) national; sick report; the speaker; the social half hour (which included "The Perils of Education", "No man in the house" and a "Pageant of Famous British Women": nothing so dramatic as today's productions of "Uncle Tom Cobbley" and "Nobody loves a fairy when she's forty"!). There was a "trading" stall every third meeting, a competition, a vote of thanks and the meeting concluded with both National Anthems.

For the past twenty years the Institute has had a very active craft group which meets in members' houses each week. In 1979 they had a stall on Mold market selling articles they had made and were able to give £100 to the Institute. More recently the group has designed and made patchwork quilts which they have given to Nightingale House, Gobowen Hospital and Riding for the Disabled as a prize for their raffles. They have also made two quilts as individual prizes for the Memorial Hall funds and the Bryneglwys show and they have a stall at the annual church fête. In all approximately £2500 has been raised for charity by this group. They have also been very successful at recent Denbigh and Flint shows by winning first, second or third places in the co-operative craft competitions, which are of a high standard.

Mrs Mowatt (left) and Mrs Jones (Belle View) at an early 1970's W.I. party in the Memorial Hall.
(Mrs Eileen Davies)

Opposite and below: A cheerful W.I. team who have just planted the anniversary bushes. The bulbs behind are part of the W.I.'s World Flowerbulb Day Prize.

Left to right: Janet Handley; Muriel Staley; Pat Thompson; Olive Williams; Jean Wilkinson; Eileen Davies.
(Janet Handley)

In 1988 Holland held a national competition for World Flowerbulb Day and Llandegla was one of twelve Institutes to win over a thousand bulbs for the village, which were given to the school children and the Darby and Joan members and planted in flower tubs for the Memorial Hall and Cenotaph. Also in 1988 they won third prize in a Federation "Diary" competition which they maintained from January to December 1988.

A garden party at Plas Tyno on September 11th 1990 to celebrate seventy-five years of the National Federation of Women's Institutes. Church bells were rung all over the country to mark this anniversary, ours being rung by Dan Jones.

Back row: Muriel Staley; Hazel Forster; Joyce Bellis; Pat Thompson; Janet Handley; Anita Hilton; Bettie Gaulton; Joan Ashworth; Eileen Davies; Irene Edwards; Vera Palmer; Dorothy Pluke.
Front row: Janet Robinson (holding picture); Olive Williams; Kathleen Mowatt; Mary McLaughlan; Peggy Swindells. *(Mr Bob McLaughlan)*

In 1994 the International and Public Affairs Committee organised a competition for Institutes *"to prepare a written and illustrated presentation of a historical and/or interesting building in the locality of your Institute"*. Four members from Llandegla were awarded first prize for

W.I. Christmas Party 1998
(Mrs Doris Jones)

the book they wrote on Bodidris, (a copy is held in the Ruthin Archives). This book has been used as a basis for a handbook for visitors to Bodidris (p.149). Mention must also be made of the bowls, darts and whist teams all of whom have played in Federation leagues or competitions.

The W.I. alternates with *Y Gymdeithas Gymraeg* (p.203) at the Annual Fête and Show when they either run a cake stall or do the refreshments to raise funds for the Memorial Hall.

And so to the next fifty years . . . . !

Merched y Wawr (*Women or Ladies of the Dawn*) *(Bet Edwards)*

The aim of the movement is to promote any cause for the benefit of women in Wales, which is considered by law to be charitable at this day in time or at any other time in the future and especially to strengthen public education and to promote Welsh culture, education and the arts in Wales. All of this is done through the medium of the Welsh language. The movement is politically impartial and religiously non-denominational.

Merched y Wawr - a happy group of prizewinners. The prize was for a scrapbook *(llyfr lloffion)*, the one held by Gaynor Jones, which represented a considerable effort by members.

Back row, left to right: Bet Edwards; Tegwen Davies; Rhiannon Robson; Meinir Beech (modestly hidden); Heulwen Roberts; Sian Lightfoot; Mair Lewis. **Front row:** Gaynor Jones (holding the book); Mary Beech; Dilys Davies (p.51). *(Mrs Bet Edwards)*

A local branch of Merched y Wawr was established on February 25th 1976 at Bryneglwys. At the very first meeting there were twelve members present and we went ahead to form a programme of activities. On July 8th 1980 we welcomed members from Llandegla and Llanarmon yn Iâl to join us and we renamed the branch as Merched y Wawr Bryneglwys a Llandegla. The meetings are held on the last Monday of every month at either the Memorial Hall, Llandegla, or the chapel vestry, Bryneglwys. A special meeting was held on April 30th 1986 at the Memorial Hall, to celebrate our tenth anniversary.

Our aim when drawing up a programme of activities is to include a variety of topics, so as to cater for everyone's interests. For example, guest speakers have talked about local history, hairdressing, ghosts, antiques, flower arranging, medicinal herbs or a day in the life of a JP, with the occasional visit to a local place of interest. We also have an annual main outing, to visit places of interest further afield, for example, Pennant Melangell, a walk around the home town of the famous Welsh novelist, Daniel Owen and Bridgemere Gardens, to name but a few. We have an evening for Welsh learners. Another annual event is the taping of the Bedol, the local monthly newspaper for the blind.

We have an annual regional festival which is held in different areas within our region of Glyn Maelor and in 1995 it was our pleasure to welcome everyone to Llandegla. The Memorial Hall was full to capacity and we enjoyed two celebrities in the field of Welsh folk songs and *Cerdd dant*, namely, Arfon Jones of Cwmtirmynach near Bala and Mair Carrington Roberts of Gwynfryn. When our branch falls within the catchment area of the National Eisteddfod of Wales or the Urdd National Eisteddfod, we contribute in a practical way by helping out in the refreshments pavilion. We enjoy competing in various competitions and have competed in the Royal Welsh Show with some success.

We celebrate Saint David's Day by going out for a meal with an invited guest speaker. In the past Dr Aled Lloyd Davies of Mold has given us a talk about local poets, bards and rhymers; Marged Jones of Frongoch, Bala, has given an account of the life of the famous Welsh harpist Nansi

Richards; Orig Williams of Ysbyty Ifan has told of life in the boxing and wrestling professions; and Reverend O R Parry of Ruthin has defined 'humour'. We also welcome children from local schools to give us a Saint David's Day concert.

Our membership has stayed about the same throughout, losing some and winning a few. We are a small, warm and friendly society and if anyone is interested in what we do, then you are more than welcome to come and join us.

We look forward to celebrating our twenty-fifth anniversary in the year 2001!

Y Gymdeithas Gymraeg *(Tegla Jones)*

The Welsh Society began in about 1924 when the Rev Alun Williams, Minister of Bethania Chapel, had the idea of starting a literary society *(Cymdeithas Lenyddol)* for members of Bethania and Pisgah Chapels. The first meeting was held in the vestry of Bethania Chapel. After World War Two the meetings moved to the Memorial Hall where it has since met every fortnight, through the winter months, without a break. Members of the Church were also welcomed. In 1957 it became the Welsh Society *(Y Gymdeithas Gymraeg)*.

Many activities are held, quizzes, debates, lectures, films, drama groups, *noson lawen*, games, ten-pin bowling, treasure hunts and so on for people of all ages. Today there are fifty adult members and twenty children. We organise events annually for different charities, raising £500 in 1999. The Welsh Society alternates with the W.I. in providing refreshments and running the cake stall at the Annual Fête, a service much appreciated by all visitors to the Fête.

Everyone works very well together and enjoys upholding Welsh traditions.

Members of the Cymdeithas Lenyddol Llandegla (the Literary Society that preceded the Welsh Society) on a trip to Aberystwyth in June 1930. Several people are mentioned elsewhere in this book (*).

Front row: Mr Jones, Beddgelert; Bob Williams, Pennant; John Lloyd Jones, Pennant; Griff Davies; Edris Parry; Will Davies.

Second row: Mrs Jones, School House; Mrs Pritchard, Tan y Bryn; Mrs R H Jones, London House; Eluned Evans, Cae Madog; Katie Hughes; Rev Alun Williams, Llys Myfyr; Adam Roberts; Joe Williams, Pennant; (Marion Jones, Bodawen); Mary Davies.

Third row: Maurice Jones, Graig; Mrs Roberts; Ellis Hughes, Llidiart Fawr; Ben Roberts; Nesta Roberts; (Mary Roberts, Green Park); Sarah J Jones, White Horse; Mrs T Parry, Arfryn Cottage; Daniel Roberts, Old Gate; Ted Edwards; J T Hughes, Rhos Isa.

Fourth row: Robert Jones; John Morris; T P Smith*, shopkeeper; Tommy Jones, Ty'n y Mynedd; Trefor Harrison*, Plough; William Roberts, Hand Inn; Hywel Edwards; Ifor A Evans, bus driver.

Back row: Sam Bloor; Meredith Evans, Garden Cottage. *(Mrs Flora Edwards)*

The Thursday Club *(Doris Jones)*

The Thursday Club was started in May 1960 by Mrs Mowatt and Mrs G R Jones. From 1960-70 it was led by Mrs Barritt (Bodidris) and Mrs Moon (Plas Tyno), and from 1970-75 by Mrs Borthwick (Old Rectory) and Mrs V Palmer (Trem y Mynydd). Since 1980 Mrs Doris Jones (Rhoslydan), assisted over the years by Mr John Bellis,

Mr Hindley, Mr Howell Edwards and Mr Chris Larkin, has led the club. At the Millennium she will have been guiding the club for the last twenty years.

Mrs Doris Jones, Club Leader, in a pensive mood at the 1995 VE Day Anniversary Party. *(Janet Handley)*

Since the club has been formed it has been fortunate in the excellent team of helpers with the refreshments and other activities which lie behind the successful social gatherings. There has been a varied programme of indoor activities over the years which have included quizzes, whist drives, bingo, slide and picture shows of the Grand Canyon, Poland, Peru, South Africa, Australia, New Zealand, China, Japan and many more. We have been lucky to benefit from other people's holidays.

Members have also been on trips organised by the club, such as a week in Ilfracombe and Torquay, and outings to Llandudno, Southport, flower festivals at Great Meols and Farndon. The club has also attended concerts at the National Eisteddfod when this was held at Mold and Abergele, and plays and musicals at Theatre Clwyd and Wrexham.

The local Gun Club has raised money for us which has been a great help with the finances. The members enjoy the Christmas Dinner which is held at The Willows, and it holds a Birthday Party every year, in May, with entertainment.

Llandegla Sports, Social and Playground Club   *(Julie Tudor)*

In 1989 Llandegla decided to enter into the Inter-Village Sports Competition and was given £100 to start them off. At the time there was no Sports and Social Club and no account to bank the money into. In 1990 the Sports and Social Club was started. The Club was very successful: the committee organised regular fund-raising events such as Fun Days and Hot-Pot Suppers to raise money. The money raised was used to buy sports equipment to practice for the Inter-Village Sports competition and to pay for the bus hired to take people to the events.

Committee members worked very hard year after year to make the club a success and the village achieved success in the annual inter-village competitions. In 1996 the same efforts were made to gather together a team for the Inter-Village Sports with a very poor response. The chairman at the time and one of the other committee members called at each person's house in the village to sign them up for another year of fun and games, but surprisingly without success. The reasons we think were that people had moved out of the village who would normally have taken part, some of the children who used to take part had grown up and were not interested any more and there were not enough young children to replace them. Reluctantly the village had to pull out and we have not entered since. The Sports and Social Club although it continued in name was not very proactive for about two years: the incentive to organise activities for the village had gone as the support faded.

However, in 1998 we were approached by some members of the committee to help them put forward plans for a children's playground and to help raise money for it. Through the constitution we changed the name to the Sports, Social and Playground Club. The plans for the playground are still being discussed and a site has been approved by the Hall Committee. We are now waiting to submit plans to gain planning permission and once this has been granted we will start to apply for grants and raise money to build the playground.

The Sports, Social and Playground Club is running very successfully with the start of a Youth Activity Club for the youngsters of the village. We are very active in the village and have a lot of plans and ideas for the future. Some of these include the completion of the playground; an annual Midsummer Night event; to re-enter the Inter-Village Sports Competition; to organise events for young and old alike. We still have a lot of work to do. To continue to run the club successfully help is always needed and as usual the present committee is made up of very busy people who give up their valuable time voluntarily to help the community of Llandegla. They work very hard and tirelessly and for this we say "thank you".

Clubs and societies for younger people

These organisations have come and gone as the number of children of a suitable age in the village has fluctuated, as has also the availability of enthusiastic leaders.

Llandegla **Guides** were founded in the 1920s. All three organisations, **Guides, Brownies and Cub Scouts** were active in the 1980s, the Brownies until 1997. Hopefully they will revive in the future.

The Brownies learning semaphore.
(Mrs Sandra Pinchbeck)

The **Church Sunday School** ran for many years, but this too has stopped for the moment.

The **Chapel Sunday School** is still going strong in Pisgah Chapel.

A Sunday School trip in the 1930s. Robert Hugh Roberts, the village blacksmith (Daniel Roberts' grandson) is in the front with the cap. *(Mrs Eileen Clarke)*

The **Youth Club** also declined and ceased, but has recently reopened and taken on a new name and a vigorous new lease of life as the **Youth Activity Club.** Julie Tudor describes the club:

"The young people of the village have said to us for a long time that they wanted to have something that was regular, fun and they could learn from. The idea of the Youth Activity Club had been talked about between members of the Sports, Social and Playground Club for about two years. Talking about it and organising it were two different things. Everyone is so busy and running a regular evening for the young people of the village takes up a lot of time and effort.

We were pushed into it a little by pressure from parents and other committee members to run an evening a week during the school summer holidays of 2000. We tried to have one evening every other week but were asked to run it every week as the young people enjoyed it so much and it gave the parents a well-earned break.

It certainly does take a lot of time and effort to continue the success of the evening especially with the dark nights drawing in and not being able to play and work outside. We try to have someone from the Denbighshire Youth Service to entertain the group and the arts and crafts have been very successful. We have also had static mountain bikes and a bouncy maze.

As we do not have Brownies or Cubs in the village any more we would like to take on the role of helping children to learn whilst they are having fun and have started to introduce new skills such as cooking. Our age range is so large from five years old upwards that it is very difficult to please all of the people all of the time and we are trying to introduce more sports as well as arts and crafts. As the club is held on a school night we cannot take the young people out in the evenings but we will in the school holidays. We have already taken them ice-skating which was a great success and hope to take them camping, training on an assault course and working on an activity centre. The list of suggestions is never ending. For the future we are hoping to start First Aid Courses, Duke of Edinburgh Awards, Mountain Bike Training and lots more...We also hope to work with the school very closely so we can complement each other's goals and aims.

Help is always needed to keep the club running and we have to have a minimum number of people to run it, otherwise we have to close for that night. This is not what we want."

The Memorial Hall

We are most fortunate to have this facility in Llandegla. The Memorial Hall is in constant use: it is a focal point for social activities such as badminton, short mat bowls, table tennis, concerts, line dancing, stage performances, youth club, lunch club and so on. More formal uses are a fortnightly surgery run by doctors from Ruthin, monthly meetings of the Community Council and other meetings such as the Sports, Social and Playground Club and the NFU.

The Memorial Hall used to be a Wesleyan Chapel. Mrs Dewhurst of Bodidris bought the Chapel in 1914, restored it, and later gave it to the village. It was opened as the Llandegla War Memorial Hall on 17th June 1918 (p.54). Despite a proposition to change its name in the 1980's being lost, the word 'War' has now been dropped from its name. Later Bodawen (p.77) and the field behind it, which is now known as the 'Hall Field', were purchased by the Hall committee. Both Bodawen and the Hall needed extensive repairs in the 1980's, and Bodawen was sold to Tai Clwyd Housing Association. Renovations to the Hall were completed in 1991 when a new kitchen, committee room, gallery, toilets and shower were built and extensive repairs to the roof and fabric of the Hall carried out.

The Memorial Hall. The two cottages next door used to be one - Bodawen. *(Janet Handley)*

The latest development has been a purpose-built pavilion in the Hall Field. Following a number of near catastrophic village fêtes with high winds on the Friday night before the show ripping off the marquee roof and various other bits and pieces, it was decided that a more substantial structure was needed. The then Chairman of the Hall committee, Mr Edward Jones J.P. of Rhoslydan, suggested a sports pavilion which could be used throughout the year for sporting activities and which would have a lockable store (enabling the committee to sell the rather unsightly green containers situated on the Memorial Hall car park). It would also house the produce show on fête day with some of the existing sheeting adapted to clad its back and front, to give it a marquee-like appearance.

Work commenced in Spring 1998 after various amendments to the original plans. It was supplied and erected by Gwynfor Jones, Ruthin, with groundwork by Arthur Black, Clawdd Newydd. At the village produce show and fête on August 29th 1998, Mr Edward Jones cut the red ribbon and declared the pavilion officially open. Further improvements were undertaken in July 2000 with the blocking in of the back wall. There are plans for a purchase of purpose-made sheeting for the 2001 fête.

Since its construction, the pavilion has housed archery, volleyball, cricket, football and netball and has been a shelter in inclement weather for children to ride bikes and for Offa's Dyke walkers to pitch their tents. However its greatest success, when it was festooned with flags and balloons and set out with tressles covered with all sorts of wonderful edibles, has been when the village celebrated the Millennium with its street party on June 24th, 2000 (p.223).

The new pavilion in the Hall Field. *(Janet Handley)*

The Hall Field and the Hall facilities are well used by campers, many of whom are walking the Offa's Dyke Path. Llandegla is a convenient overnight stop before tackling the Clwydians going north or the Eglwyseg and Berwyns going south. The Offa's Dyke Path just goes past most villages: Llandegla is one of a very few villages where the Path goes through the middle.

The Memorial Hall is owned by the village as a registered charity. It is managed by a committee made up of elected representatives from each village organisation that makes use of the Hall and some co-opted members. Income comes from hire of the rooms, the Annual Fête and other events. Maintenance is under the wing of the buildings subcommittee. A part-time caretaker is now employed by the committee for the various domestic tasks that keep the Hall clean, neat and tidy. It has a very close relationship with the school which makes use of it for indoor sports, school dinners and other school activities.

In 1993 the Memorial Hall was presented with a certificate and a cheque for £100 as first prize in Clwyd's Best Kept Village Hall competition. Not only were the judges impressed with the state of the building (including the spotless kitchen!), but they were also impressed with the excellent use made of the facilities by local organisations.

In the past the Hall Committee has been particularly fortunate in two of its members: Mrs Dilys Davies (pp.51, 189) and Mr William Owen. Mrs Davies was much more than the caretaker: she was on the committee for well over twenty years, her dedication ensuring the smooth running of the Hall. Mr Owen was treasurer for well over thirty years. At the last Llandegla fête he was presented with a large illustrated plaque to mark his retirement. This plaque celebrated his long-standing commitment to the Memorial Hall, school and Llandegla Church to which he gave many years of invaluable service and counsel.

The plaque presented to Mr Owen to mark his retirement as Treasurer. in 1999.

Events are held which are important for the social life of the village but also raise

212

The Nativity Play
in the Memorial
Hall, 1981.
(Mr Tegla Jones)

Barry the commen-
tator reports on the
progress of the
ducks during the
1994 Boxing Day
Duck Race. This
annual event, first
held in the late
1980's, is a good
way to blow away
those Christmas
cobwebs!
(Janet Handley)

The spectators on
the bridge have all
been well supplied
with mince pies
and coffee.
(Janet Handley)

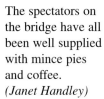

funds for the Hall. These include the Christmas Fayre and the Boxing Day Duck Race. However the most significant event is the Fête and Show which has been held annually since 1957 (p.216).

Social Activities: The 1928 Grand Bazaar

Events have often been planned to raise money for various causes within the village: the Annual Fête for the Memorial Hall and the Christmas Fair for Llandegla Church are two examples. These are also important as social events. In 1928 a Grand Bazaar was held to raise money for Pisgah Chapel (pp.186-187). The aim of this bazaar was to liquidate a remaining debt of £50 (about £1,700 today) which had been incurred by the installation of new heating apparatus, the painting of the chapel and the need to pay off an old debt. An "official" twenty-six-page handbook was printed for this event. Through its general information and the fifty advertisements it gives a flavour of what it was like to live in Llandegla around seventy years ago.

At this time Captain and Mrs Dewhurst lived in Bodidris and it is no surprise to note that the Bazaar was opened on Thursday 2nd February 1928 by Mrs G P Dewhurst in The War Memorial Hall. The announcement of this task was preceded by a quotation: *"A good beginning makes a good ending"*. The Bazaar was made up of several 'Stalls', each of these listed in the handbook with the names of the people who manned the stall. There was a quotation for each of the stalls:

for the **Work Stall:** *"A little chaff is very well, A little harmless laughter, But patronage and £. s. d., is really what we're after"*;

the **Farm Produce and Pound Stall:** *"We have goods that you require, You have the cash we desire"*;

the **Fancy Work Stall:** *"From early till late our fingers are nimble, We have gathered this store by our needle and thimble"*;

the **Crockery Stall:** *"Do buy" (The Merchant of Venice)*;

the **Confectionery Stall:** *"Women are more powerful to persuade"*;

the **Refreshment Stall:** *"Sit down and feed and welcome to our table"*;

and finally the Miscellaneous Stall: "Here are wares well worth possessing, And every purchase brings a blessing".

According to the advertisements, the shops in Llandegla offered a wide range of goods, despite the "good shoping" in Coedpoeth, Wrexham, Treuddyn, Graigfechan and Ruthin (Mold did not appear in the Handbook). Fewer people would then have had their own transport and travelling to shop would not have been easy:

- The 'noted establishment' of T P Smith, Pioneer Stores, Llandegla, 'Grocer and Provision Dealer, Corn and Flour Merchant'... 'fresh and carefully selected delicious flavoured bacon and prime Cheshire cheese always in stock. For QUALITY and VALUE we are undoubtedly pre-eminent'. Regular delivery by motor van (p.83);

- John Harrison, Family Butcher, offered QUALITY, VALUE AND SERVICE;

- E S Harrison of Yale Garage, situated on the present Plough car park (p.97), sold Hercules cycles for £3.15.0d, fully guaranteed and Wireless Sets are Cheaper!! Complete VALVE SETS from £3.15.0d (about £107) all guaranteed, any set supplied on 7 days free trial, ask for demonstration;

- Roberts Bros (one of these being Mr Tegla Jones' grandfather, p.45) were Tailors and Drapers and made suits to order;

- The Post Office Stores were run by Jones Brothers and their telephone number was No. 1, Llandegla;

- The final 'local' advert was George Edward Jones of The Crown Hotel, a Haulage Contractor and Taxi. Distance no object, estimates free. His taxi can be seen outside the Crown in 1937 (p.100).

In addition to the advertisements each handbook was numbered and a prize of seven shillings and sixpence was given to the holder of the programme bearing the Lucky Number. This practice is still carried out with our Fête programmes.

Llandegla Fête and Show

There had been a fête in the field behind The Hand for many years. In 1957, Mr Edmund Edge from Chweleiriog Goch was chatting in the shop with the proprietor, Mr Howard, and said we ought to have a flower and produce show alongside the fête. Mr Howard took the idea to the Hall Committee of which he was a member. They reluctantly agreed to give it a try and a show committee was set up comprising Mr Howard, Mr T P Smith, Mr Tom Jones, Mr Edge and Mrs Mowatt. A marquee was hired, Mr Barritt of Bodidris had the first schedules printed and gave the prize money, and the Show was launched.

Four gentlemen attending the very first Llandegla Fête and Show: Mr Ted Edge, Mr John Robson, Mr Ted Ellis, Mr Matthew Robson. *(Mrs Marjorie Edge)*

In 1963 the Young Farmers were asked to run the Show, which they did until falling numbers made it impractical to do so. Meanwhile the Hall Committee had purchased Bodawen field and the Fête and Show moved there. Mrs Marjorie Edge undertook the organisation of the Show as secretary, with many dedicated helpers over the years. The present secretary is Mrs Sandra Williams-Blythen.

The cost of hiring a marquee kept steadily rising and eating into the profits, so Mr Ken Bellis and Mr Peter Bennett got together and built a framework of redundant scaffolding poles over which canvas was stretched (total cost £150). This served successfully for many years until the present pavilion was built and opened in 1999.

The Rose Queen, Haf Jones, at the 1981 Fête. *(Mr Tegla Jones)*

The official opening is followed by the crowning of the Rose Queen (one of the local children). The pavilion houses an exhibition of local grown flowers and vegetables, art, photography, handicrafts, cookery, wine and children's competitions. On the Hall Field side shows, a local band and an excellent refreshment tent make for an enjoyable afternoon. An evening event rounds off the day and there is community singing in the church or chapel led by Mr Tegla Jones.

The Show has gone from strength to strength and has an impressive array of trophies. Even though the standard of entries is very high, it was meant as a fun show which anyone could enter, and this has always been maintained. Long may it continue!

Some past sports activities

As with societies for the younger generation, the vigour of sports activities depended on the availability of men and women to take part, the enthusiasm of one or more individuals to get everyone to work together and the opportunity to compete with like-minded people or teams. Unfortunately these factors do not always come together at the same time, so these activities tend to come and go.

Llandegla fielded a team in the local **Football Summer League**. Funds were boosted by raffles for which prizes were often cigarettes, chocolates and even eggs which had been donated. In 1957 the referee's fee was seven shillings and sixpence per match. A new football cost two pounds sixteen shillings and the laundry bill was £2. (£1 then was worth about £13 now).

The Llandegla team came to an end about forty years ago. It was at a time when farms were being amalgamated, so there were fewer young lads on the farm who were available to take part.

The first **All-Wales Festival of Sport** was staged at Aberystwyth by the National Federation of Young Farmers' Clubs. The badminton mixed doubles was won by Colin Hindley and Hazel Edwards from Llandegla. The tradition lives on: badminton is still played in the Memorial Hall each Wednesday.

Haydn Edwards (Team Manager 1988-92) writes:

> *The **Inter-Village Sports Competition** was formed in 1988. A letter was sent out to each Community Council in Glyndŵr by the District Council inviting each community to form a sports team. The Sports Council for Wales were to sponsor the first competition with prize money of £100 for the winners to be spent on sports equipment for the village, plus medals for first (gold), second (silver) and third (bronze).*
>
> *Llandegla Community Council decided to take an interest in the competition but first they had to appoint a manager to run the team, which they did. Interest from the Llandegla community was overwhelming, with sports for all ages from five to ninety-five years. Some of the sports were traditional: football (men's and*

ladies'), tug-of-war (men's and ladies'), rounders (mixed), table tennis, swimming, badminton, relay running. But there were also some sports which were unheard of at the time by many in Llandegla: short mat bowls, short tennis and unihoc.

The first heat was held in early September, 1988. A fifty-one seater coach was hired, T-shirts with "Llandegla Sports Team" printed on the front, purchased for all team members by the licensees of the Crown Hotel, Mike and Barbara Conway, and off we went to Brynhyfryd School, Ruthin. After competing all that Sunday afternoon we were successful; and qualified for the final held later that month. We came up against the winners of the other three heats. After another exciting afternoon, Llandegla were just pipped at the post by Llanrheadr ym Mochnant by half a point, and had to be content with the runners-up position.

This made us even more determined to be successful the following year, 1989. New T-shirts were ordered, this time sponsored by the Crown Hotel and H Davies and Sons (Haulage) (Tegid Davies, Pontystyllod). Off we went again, some on the George Edwards coach from Bwlchgwyn and some in cars, with a team of about sixty children and adults for the community of Llandegla to improve on the previous year. After being successful once again in the first heat we were destined for the final for the second year running.

After competing in a close-run competition against the other villages from the Glyndŵr district, one of them being possibly our biggest rivals, Llanarmon yn Iâl, we were this time successful and Llandegla became the winners of the 1989 Inter-Village Sports

Competition. Celebrations were held that night in the Crown with most of the team turning up. The Cup was displayed in the Post Office window and a party

The celebrations continue in the Crown: Haydn Edwards in his team manager's shirt and Medwyn Owen enjoy a pint while Simon White looks on. (Haydn Edwards)

219

The team that made it in 1989, wearing their winners' badges, relaxing as they wait for the formal team photograph to be taken.

Top row (visible): Jim Thompson; Phil Clark; Ken Staley

Second row: Daphne McGwire; Marion Allen; Gill Dyke; Muriel Staley; Olive Williams; Pat Thompson; Neville Allen

Third row: David McGwire; Michael Robinson; Julie Davies; Sandra Williams Blythen; Carol Edge; Sarah White; Janet Handley; Kath Evans; Louie Hughes

Front row: Christine Hughes; Jo Oliver; Margaret Mooney; Haydn Edwards; Denise Lloyd; Fleur Davies   *(Haydn Edwards)*

Enjoyment continues for the younger generation as they replace lost energy. On the left, Pierce Hughes and Ieuan White; on the right, John Lloyd, in company with other successful junior team members. *(Haydn Edwards)*

held in the Memorial Hall with photos of the team taken and also a showing of the video of the day's events.

The following two years saw Llandegla reach the Final, being runner-up again in 1990. Llandegla continued to enter the competition until 1992. The Table Tennis Club and the Short Mat Bowls Club were formed as a result of the Inter-Village Sports, and also badminton in the Memorial Hall revived. The Sports and Social Club was also formed with the help of the prize money. I was privileged and honoured to have been part of those teams, especially on that day in 1989."

Short mat bowls has carried on since its introduction for the Inter-Village Sports Competition. The standard has continued to improve, the Llandegla team winning the local league in 1997 and 1998.

Two more local success stories

Caroline Hughes is just one of the younger generation in the village who have taken their enthusiasm beyond a passing interest to excel. Caroline, of Dafarn Dywyrch, is the great-great-great-granddaughter of the Rev.

Caroline Hughes of Dafarn Dywyrch *(Mr Jim Hughes)*

Samuel Evans (p.186). She won the Welsh Junior Tennis Championship at Cardiff in 1978 and 1979 (under 12); 1980 (under 14); 1982 and 1983 (under 16); and 1984 (under 18). In 1987 at Swansea she was crowned Senior Champion of Wales in the Ladies' Singles, Ladies Doubles and Mixed Doubles. At 14, she was the youngest player to win the North Wales Ladies Open. She has represented Wales at international level for both junior and senior teams on numerous occasions. She played first lady for the Neston club, Wirral, for fifteen years and has been captain for the last five years.

221

John Lightfoot is a well-known sheepdog handler who has won many local and national trials. He has lived at Pentre Isaf since 1958. He has won the North Wales Open Championship and represented his country in the TV programme *One man and his dog,* where he twice reached the final. With his dogs Black and Jet he won the Welsh National at Dolgellau in 1991; reached the qualifying round of the Farmers' Championship; ran in the International Trials at Mostyn in 1995 and the Centenary Trials at Viviod; and twice won the Subaru Championship at Pwllglas. He breeds and trains his own dogs and has judged both locally, nationally and internationally in Holland and Belgium in 1998.

John Lightfoot with 'Black'
(four years old) *(Beryl Lightfoot)*

Celebrating the Millennium

There had been much discussion in the village about how to celebrate the new millennium. One option was to have a bar in the pavilion and entertainment in the Memorial Hall (no alcohol may be sold in the Hall as it is an old chapel), but there was the possibility of bad weather and perhaps too few people to create the right atmosphere. There was also some uncertainly which New Year's Eve to celebrate: 1999-2000 or 2000-2001. It was decided to have a street party in the summer instead. As it turned out, there were celebrations on both New Year's Eves, so the year 2000 was topped and tailed with a bit in the middle!

The first Millennium New Year's Eve

About two weeks before the New Year, a beacon was unexpectedly donated to the village by British Gas, conveniently powered by gas (naturally!). This was sited on the grass opposite the Crown Hotel. Within a fortnight money was raised and arrangements made. A hotpot supper was prepared, fireworks bought, safety ropes erected, marshalls organised and all was ready for the beacon to be lit in front of an

The moment of ignition. Dr Bickford is holding the wand up to the beacon which has just burst into flames
(Dionne Bhalla)

expectant crowd - but no match! Eventually a source of ignition was found: a wand consisting of a long pole with paraffin-soaked cloth wound around one end. Dr Bickford applied the burning wand to the beacon and flames rose up into the evening. A large crowd of all ages enjoyed the fireworks and warmed their insides with the hotpot supper. Many then crowded into the Crown which had a real family atmosphere and a welcome buffet. Later, on the stroke of midnight, everyone took a celebratory drink outside to view another firework display, and all sang *Auld Lang Syne* around the beacon. The party continued into the early hours: the beacon was still going strong when the last of the revellers left at eight o'clock in the morning.

The Millennium street party and pram push.
(Dionne Bhalla and David Alcock)

The street party was held on June Saturday 24th 2000, the nearest Saturday to Midsummer's Day. It began with a procession through the

The King and Queen with Uncle Bob: Steven Hampson, Kyza Edwards and Bob Jones *(Dionne Bhalla)*

village led by our Millennium King and Queen, Steven Hampson and Kyza Edwards, followed by brightly dressed prams and spectators sporting fancy dress. The Millennium beacon was lit and 'Uncle' Bob Jones and Mrs Edge crowned the King and Queen. Then the First Llandegla Pram Push began.

The pram push on the day of the Millennium street party was planned as an event to incorporate all generations and provide the crowds with entertainment prior to the street party feast later. Remarkably, many of the 'pillars' of village life had been coerced into pram teams by the organisers, and these unwitting stalwarts gave us the base around which to build the event. The list of teams grew as village rumours got around, giving all the chance to show their general knowledge, team spirit and physical abilities.Teams prepared themselves as usual: last-minute phone calls were received asking for the definition of a 'pram' (basically anything manually powered!). Originally teams were supposed to be a three-generation family group, but as usual chaos was the rule of the day! Costumes ranged wide including crocodile suits, nappies and dummies, flat caps and moustaches, winged horses, doctors and nurses. Challenges were devised around everyday things here in Llandegla: shopping, education, country walks, village sports, baby feeding and the great water mains replacement of 2000!

After such an exhausting, enterprising, energetic and entertaining event, everyone descended on the delicious buffet in the pavilion, provided by the community (everyone brought a contribution). There was a fancy

All the children in fancy
dress on the pavilion stage
(Dionne Bhalla)

…and some older
contestants!
(Dionne Bhalla)

dress competition for adults and children, with all kinds of fanciful creations, which was eventually won by an Arabian princess (Sara Campbell) and Little Bo Peep (Siobhan Gledhill). Next a local magician, Maria Garwell, entertained the children (and the adults) with a magic show and all the children received a celebratory goody bag.

In the committee room of the Hall, a photographic display showing Llandegla through the years proved to be a very popular attraction (the photographs displayed are all in this book).

Unfortunately everyone enjoyed themselves so much, winners, losers, forgers and shoplifters alike, that we were asked to run another Pram

Push in 2001. *(Editor's note: I'm hoping we haven't started this for a whole millennium. I certainly won't be here to see it through to full term.)*

The second Millennium New Year's Eve *(Julie Tudor)*

Six o'clock on New Year's Eve 2000 and the snow had turned to slush, the wind howled and the rain came down. It was cold and very slippery underfoot but this did not deter the locals from creating a lively atmosphere at the Plough. They waited, dressed in warm winter coats and wellies, to see the Millennium Beacon being lit again by a local sports celebrity. Nicola Tustain from Bryneglwys won two gold medals and one bronze medal for dressage in the equestrian events at the Para-Olympics in Sydney, Australia. She braved the bad weather and lit the beacon at seven o'clock, which then burned till 6.00am. As the night progressed the fun increased: Hazel and Richard put on their usual wonderful buffet and people ate, drank and were merry well into the night. As well as everyone having a good time, money was raised to share between the school and an appeal in Wrexham for a children's cancer care hospital.

***

We have reached the end of our efforts to mark the new millennium with a record, however partial and incomplete, of our village and parish. Let the last word go to our editor, Phil Clark:

"It will have become obvious to the reader that this book has indeed been written by the inhabitants of Llandegla. Both the wide range of photographs and the text have come from many people. Some have written their knowledge and reminicences as a substantive contribution, others recalled their memories verbally. I have been greatly encouraged by the enthusiasm of our residents and the willing help received from people and public bodies that reside outside our Parish. It has been a fascinating experience and I am most grateful for having been given this opportunity."

11. THE END BIT

Acknowledgements

This has been the most difficult part to put together. So many people have contributed to the book in one way or another, I hope that everyone has had a mention, and can only apologise if there is anyone who feels that they have been left out. Contributions have varied from substantial writing that has formed the foundation for one or more sections to verbal comments that have filled in a gap in our knowledge or led to a new line of inquiry. Much of the writing in this book is a blending together of material from several people and resources. Tegla Jones, Janet Handley and Janet Robinson have provided substantial chunks of text which have been treated in this manner. Where a piece has been written by one author this has been acknowledged individually, as have photographs. There is much more to a book than the writing. Others listed have worked in the background to assisting the gathering of material, putting the text into a suitable form for publication, and working to obtain finance and looking after the business side of publication: Sheila Byrne, Ian Robinson, Lou and Maureen Thompson, Audrey Lockyer, Fleur Davies and Janet Strivens, and valued support from Mr William Owen, as well as many others. However, without the help of all of the people listed below, this book would not have happened.

It is a matter of the deepest regret that a few of the people listed below are no longer with us as they passed away during the time that this was being written.

Mr & Mrs David Alcock	Mr Dan Jones
Mrs K Beech	Mrs Doris Jones
Mr Tudur Beech	Mr Edward Jones
Mr & Mrs Ken Bellis	Mrs Sylvia Jones
Mrs Dionne Bhalla	Mr Tegla Jones
Dr J Bickford	Mr Roy Keogh

Mrs Sheila Byrne
Mrs Eileen Clarke
Mr John Clemence
Mr Simon Clemence
Mr & Mrs Cottier
Mrs Dilys Davies
Mrs Eileen Davies
Miss Fleur Davies
Mr Richard Davies
Mr Trefor Davies
Mr Robin Dyke
Mrs Marjorie Edge
Mrs Bet Edwards
Mrs Flora Edwards
Mr Fred Edwards
Mr Haydn Edwards
Mrs Irene Edwards
Mr Maldwyn Evans
Mrs Betty Forster
Miss Eunice Francis
Mr Doug Garside
Mrs Edna Goulden
The Reverend Brian Hall
Miss Janet Handley
Mr Carl Hellyn
Mr Clive Hindley
Mr Colin Hindley
Mrs Menna Hubbard
Mrs Gwen M Hughes
Mr Bob Jones
Ms Gill Kingston
Mrs Mabel Lewis

Mrs Beryl Lightfoot
Mrs Rhianon Lloyd
Mrs Audrey Lockyer
Mr Malone
Mrs Carol Matthews
Mr & Mrs Alan Moore
Mr Elwyn Owen
Mr Llywelyn Owen
Mr Medwyn Owen
Mr William Owen
Mr David Penman
Mrs Susan Percival
Mrs Sandra Pinchbeck
Mr Derek Rennie
Mrs Linda Roberts
Miss Ann Robinson
Mrs Janet Robinson
Mr Ian Robinson
Mr Bob Robson
Mr Alan Scrivner
Ms Janet Strivens
Mrs Linda Sylvia
Mr Lou Thompson
Mrs Maureen Thompson
Mrs Julie Tudor
Mrs Norma Weston
Mrs Jean Wilkinson
Mrs Sandra Williams-Blythen
Mrs Dorothy Williams
Mr David Wylie
Mrs Juliette Wylie

Llandegla is part of a much larger community, so the help that has come from outside the parish has been most supportive during the preparation of this book.

Relatively frequent visits have been made to the Record Offices in Ruthin and Hawarden, and the Library in Wrexham. The willing assistance given by the staff on each occasion has been much appreciated. Other organisations have also been most helpful in dealing with questions that must have seemed to be out of the ordinary: the Record Offices in Dolgellau and Chester, the Library in Bala, the Dee Valley Water Company in Rhostyllen.

The following have also contributed directly or indirectly to this book, their input adding strength to the content.

Dr Paul Evans
Mr Frank Jones, Llangollen
Mr Derek Williams
Mrs Kathleen White
Mr P C Evans, Bryn Cowlyd Water Treatment Works (Dŵr Cymru)
Mr Barry Hamilton, Shire Hall, Mold.
Mr Gerally Nash, Welsh Mills Society
Mrs Fiona Gale, County Archaeologist, Ruthin
Mr Peter Roberts, Dee Water Company
Mr Rob Jones, Merseyside Tramway Preservation Society
Mr Spencer Hughes
Mr David Crane, Llangollen

References

Though this book is largely a history written by those who are part of it, the sources below have been consulted as well in order to fill in some of the detail.

Books and booklets

Avent, Richard (1983) *Castles of the Princes of Gwynedd* HMSO
Bickford, H (1994) *The Wild Girl.*
Borrow, George (1862) *Wild Wales* World Classics 1951 Edn, OUP
Cathcart King (1997) *Castles in Wales and the Marches.*
    University of Wales Press
Clwyd Record Office (1978) *The Tithe War*
Crane, David (2000) *Walks through the history of rural Llangollen,*
    Wrexham: Bridge Books
Dawkins, W.Boyd (1874) *Cave Hunting* Macmillen and Co
Harley, J.R. (1975) *Ordnance Survey Maps: A descriptive manual*
    Southampton Ordnance Society
Holland, R. (1992) *Haunted Clwyd*, Gwasg Garreg Gwalch
Hubbard, E (1986) *The buildings of Wales*: *Clwyd (Denbighshire and
    Flintshire)* Penguin Books/University of Wales Press
Jones, Anthea (2000) *A thousand years of the English parish*, Windrush
    Press
Jones, T (1997) *Rioting in North East Wales, 1536 - 1918.* Bridge Books
Knowles, D S & Parkin, B E (1978) *Just one Parish.* D Seed Knowles.
Oliver, R. (1993) *Ordnance Survey Maps,* The Charles Close Society
Plessy Radar (1971) *The Dee Weather Radar Project*, The Plessey
    Company Ltd
Price-Jones, F (1952) *The story of Denbighshire through its castles.* Gee
    & Sons Ltd.
Pritchard, T W (undated) *The Parish Church of St Garmon, Llanarmon
    yn Iâl, Denbighshire.*
Richards, M C (1969) *Welsh administrative and territorial units.*
    University of Wales Press

Roberts, D. (1999) *The old villages of Denbighshire and Flintshire,* Gwasg Garreg Press

Royal Commission (1921) *Inventory for Denbighshire*

Sherratt, G (2000) *An illustrated history of Llangollen.* Ceiriog Press.

Smith, Peter (1975) *Houses of the Welsh Countryside (HMSO)*

Thomas, Rev. DR (1874) *History of the Diocese of St Asaph (1st Edn.)* Parker

Tilhill Economic Forestry (2001) *Coed Llandegla Management and Design Plan 2000-2010,* Tilhill Economic Forestry

Williams. D (1999) *Rebecca Riots.* University of Wales Press.

Womens Institute, Llandegla Branch (1994) *Bodidris,* Llandegla.

Wrexham and East Denbighshire Water Company (1964) Booklet to celebrate the centenary of the Company.

William, E (1993) *Home-made homes.* National Museum of Wales.

Whitaker's Almanac (1999). The Stationery Office.

Newspapers, Magazines and Journals

Denbighshire Free Press, July 11, 1986.

'FG' (2000) "The Story of St Collen", *The Courier,* April 2000

Davies, E C (1933-34) "Achub nerth dŵr - Cymro wrth y gwaith", *Y Ford Gron* 4 (11) : 248

Gwasg y Dywysogaeth, Wrexham.

Jones, R B (1985) "On the Welsh drovers' trail", *Country Quest,* November 1985

Marriott, F (1986) "Long road to the South", *Country Quest,* March 1986

Marriott, F (1982) "Eagle eyes on traffic watch" *The Chronicle,* July 30th 1982

Maud, T B & Jenkins, M (1987) *The Tramways of Birkenhead and Wallasey,* The Light Rail Transit Association

Owen, D (1970) "Fowls for falling sickness", *Country Quest,* August 1970.

Wrexham Leader, 12 April 1996.

Maps and related documents

Dates related to these maps are quoted in the text. These dates can only be treated as approximate with reference to features on the ground as survey work will normally have been done a few years before the publication of the map.

1667 Denbigh Comitatus pars olim Ordovicum
1740 Map of mountain land in the two hundreds of Bromfield and Yale co. Denbigh, done for Sir Robert Grosvenor, Baronet. Surveyed by Thomas Bleasdale.
1740 (Copy by George Bellis c. 1864. 8 inches to 1 mile).
Calveley, J. (1812) *Llandegla Parish Boundary* (Handwritten document)
c. 1847 Enclosure map: Allotments in the Parish of Llandeglae.
1847 Map of the Parish of Llandegla in the County of Denbighshire, Robert Perry, Chirk.
1850 Map of the proposed railway line between Brymbo and Ruthin
1879 Ordnance Survey six inches to one mile, Sheet XXXIV
1883 Index to the Ordance Survey of Denbighshire, six inches to one mile.
1912 Ordance Survey County Series 1:2500. *(These maps were used to identify fields and properties when the Dewhurst family sold the Bodidris estate in 1958)*
1963 Ordnance Survey six inches to one mile, sheets SJ 15 SE; SJ 14 NE; SJ 24 NW.
1982 Ordnance Survey Pathfinder Map 1:25000, Sheet 805
1989 Ordnance Survey Pathfinder Map 1:25000, Sheet 788
1991 Ordnance Survey Pathfinder Map 1:25000, Sheet 806
1992 Ordnance Survey Pathfinder Map 1:25000, Sheet 789
2000 Ordnance Survey Landplan, 1:10000, coordinates 319758/352187.
2000 Ordnance Survey Explorer Map, 1:25000, Sheet 256.

Index of names

Index of places

ESGOBAETH LLANELWY
Llandegla

Bu farw'r cymeriad annwyl Mr Daniel Jones, clochydd y plwyf am 60 mlynedd ac yn dilyn ei dad a'i daid yn y swydd anrhydeddus honno. Na nid swydd chwaith ond galwedigaeth. Bu'n gefn i saith Rheithor yn ei amser, a phob un â gair da iddo ac yn gwerthfawrogi ei gymorth parod ar bob achlysur.

Hyfrydwch oedd gweld yr eglwys yn llawn o bobl o bob enwad i'r gwasanaeth o ddiolch am fywyd a gwasanaeth Daniel Jones. Arweiniwyd gan y Parchg Brian Hall a darllenwyd y llith `Tynged y Cyfiawn' (Doethineb Solomon 3: 1-9) gan William Owen, Warden y Rheithor. Ychydig flynyddoedd yn ôl, ac yng nghwmni Huw Jones yr esgob cynorthwyol bryd hynny, cawsom gyfle i ddiolch i'r clochydd rhadlon am 50 mlynedd o wasanaeth diflino i Eglwys Dduw. Ar yr achlysur hwnnw canodd Beryl Lightfoot nifer o benillion iddo, gan ei gyfarch fel gwr clên a chyfaill ffyddlon, cymwynaswr parod ei wên, wrth ei fodd yn smocio'i getyn, ac un hoff o draddodiadau a hen arferion yr eglwys. Ac ychwanegodd,

Ceidw'r eglwys dan ei adain
Gwylia bopeth ddaw i'w rhan;
Ceidw lygad ar y Person
Gwnaiff yn siwr na dderbyn gam.

Diolch i Dduw am bob coffa ohono. Heddwch i'w lwch.

W. O. Ruthun